Modern Critical Interpretations

D. H. Lawrence's
Sons and Lovers

Modern Critical Interpretations

The Oresteia
Beowulf
The General Prologue to
   The Canterbury Tales
The Pardoner's Tale
The Knight's Tale
The Divine Comedy
Exodus
Genesis
The Gospels
The Iliad
The Book of Job
Volpone
Doctor Faustus
The Revelation of St.
   John the Divine
The Song of Songs
Oedipus Rex
The Aeneid
The Duchess of Malfi
Antony and Cleopatra
As You Like It
Coriolanus
Hamlet
Henry IV, Part I
Henry IV, Part II
Henry V
Julius Caesar
King Lear
Macbeth
Measure for Measure
The Merchant of Venice
A Midsummer Night's
   Dream
Much Ado About
   Nothing
Othello
Richard II
Richard III
The Sonnets
Taming of the Shrew
The Tempest
Twelfth Night
The Winter's Tale
Emma
Mansfield Park
Pride and Prejudice
The Life of Samuel
   Johnson
Moll Flanders
Robinson Crusoe
Tom Jones
The Beggar's Opera
Gray's Elegy
Paradise Lost
The Rape of the Lock
Tristram Shandy
Gulliver's Travels

Evelina
The Marriage of Heaven
   and Hell
Songs of Innocence and
   Experience
Jane Eyre
Wuthering Heights
Don Juan
The Rime of the Ancient
   Mariner
Bleak House
David Copperfield
Hard Times
A Tale of Two Cities
Middlemarch
The Mill on the Floss
Jude the Obscure
The Mayor of
   Casterbridge
The Return of the Native
Tess of the D'Urbervilles
The Odes of Keats
Frankenstein
Vanity Fair
Barchester Towers
The Prelude
The Red Badge of
   Courage
The Scarlet Letter
The Ambassadors
Daisy Miller, The Turn
   of the Screw, and
   Other Tales
The Portrait of a Lady
Billy Budd, Benito Cer-
   eno, Bartleby the Scriv-
   ener, and Other Tales
Moby-Dick
The Tales of Poe
Walden
Adventures of
   Huckleberry Finn
The Life of Frederick
   Douglass
Heart of Darkness
Lord Jim
Nostromo
A Passage to India
Dubliners
A Portrait of the Artist as
   a Young Man
Ulysses
Kim
The Rainbow
Sons and Lovers
Women in Love
1984
Major Barbara

Man and Superman
Pygmalion
St. Joan
The Playboy of the
   Western World
The Importance of Being
   Earnest
Mrs. Dalloway
To the Lighthouse
My Antonia
An American Tragedy
Murder in the Cathedral
The Waste Land
Absalom, Absalom!
Light in August
Sanctuary
The Sound and the Fury
The Great Gatsby
A Farewell to Arms
The Sun Also Rises
Arrowsmith
Lolita
The Iceman Cometh
Long Day's Journey Into
   Night
The Grapes of Wrath
Miss Lonelyhearts
The Glass Menagerie
A Streetcar Named
   Desire
Their Eyes Were
   Watching God
Native Son
Waiting for Godot
Herzog
All My Sons
Death of a Salesman
Gravity's Rainbow
All the King's Men
The Left Hand of
   Darkness
The Brothers Karamazov
Crime and Punishment
Madame Bovary
The Interpretation of
   Dreams
The Castle
The Metamorphosis
The Trial
Man's Fate
The Magic Mountain
Montaigne's Essays
Remembrance of Things
   Past
The Red and the Black
Anna Karenina
War and Peace

These and other titles in preparation

Modern Critical Interpretations

D. H. Lawrence's
Sons and Lovers

Edited and with an introduction by

Harold Bloom
Sterling Professor of the Humanities
Yale University

Chelsea House Publishers ◊ *1988*

NEW YORK ◊ NEW HAVEN ◊ PHILADELPHIA

© 1988 by Chelsea House Publishers, a division
of Chelsea House Educational Communications, Inc.,
95 Madison Avenue, New York, NY 10016
345 Whitney Avenue, New Haven, CT 06511
5068B West Chester Pike, Edgemont, PA 19028

Introduction © 1988 by Harold Bloom

Printed and bound in the United States of America

10 9 8 7 6 5 4 3 2 1

∞The paper used in this publication meets the minimum
requirements of the American National Standard for Permanence
of Paper for Printed Library Materials, Z39.48–1984.

Library of Congress Cataloging-in-Publication Data
D.H. Lawrence's Sons and lovers / edited and with an
introduction by Harold Bloom.
        p.   cm. — (Modern critical interpretations)
    "A representative selection of the best critical interpreta-
tions of D.H. Lawrence's novel, Sons and lovers"—P.
    Bibliography: p.
    Includes index.
    Contents: On Sons and lovers / Dorothy Van Ghent — The
son and the artist / H.M. Daleski — Portrait of Miriam / Louis
L. Martz — The vital self / Calvin Bedient — Speaking of Paul
Morel : voice, unity and meaning in Sons and lovers / Daniel
R. Schwarz—Eros and metaphor in Sons and lovers / Mark
Kinkead-Weekes — Reading Sons and lovers / E.P. Shrubb —
Paul's passion / Gavriel Ben-Ephraim — The artist as psycholo-
gist / Daniel J. Schneider.
    ISBN 1-55546-024-0 (alk. paper) : $24.50
    1. Lawrence, D. H. (David Herbert), 1885–1930. Sons and lovers.
  [1. Lawrence, D. H. (David Herbert), 1885–1930. Sons and lovers.
  2. English literature—History and criticism.]   I. Bloom, Harold.
  II. Title: DH Lawrence's Sons and lovers.   III. Series.
PR6023.A93S667   1988
823'.912--dc19
                                                    87-17831
                                                       CIP
                                                        AC

ontents

Editor's Note / vii

Introduction / 1
HAROLD BLOOM

On *Sons and Lovers* / 5
DOROTHY VAN GHENT

The Son and the Artist / 23
H. M. DALESKI

Portrait of Miriam / 47
LOUIS L. MARTZ

The Vital Self / 71
CALVIN BEDIENT

Speaking of Paul Morel: Voice, Unity,
and Meaning in *Sons and Lovers* / 79
DANIEL R. SCHWARZ

Eros and Metaphor in *Sons and Lovers* / 103
MARK KINKEAD-WEEKES

Reading *Sons and Lovers* / 109
E. P. SHRUBB

Paul's Passion / 131
GAVRIEL BEN-EPHRAIM

The Artist as Psychologist / 143
DANIEL J. SCHNEIDER

Chronology / 155

Contributors / 159

Bibliography / 161

Acknowledgments / 165

Index / 167

Editor's Note

This book brings together a representative selection of the best critical interpretations of D. H. Lawrence's novel *Sons and Lovers*. The essays are reprinted here in the chronological order of their original publication. I am grateful to Johann Pillai for his assistance in editing this volume.

My introduction considers both the aesthetic limitations of *Sons and Lovers* and its presages of Lawrence's later achievement in the novel. Dorothy Van Ghent begins the chronological sequence of criticism with her early essay on symbolism in *Sons and Lovers*, juxtaposing the forces of flowers and of darkness.

In H. M. Daleski's classic reading of the novel, the breach in Lawrence's own nature between male and female principles is strikingly delineated. A spirited defense of the representation of Miriam as being essentially positive is made by Louis Martz.

Calvin Bedient centers upon Lawrence's early vitalism, heroic in its polemic against positivism. Lawrence's psyche rather than his intentions is mimed in the novel, according to Daniel R. Schwarz. Some of the metaphorical perplexities of Lawrence's ways of representing sexual relationships are outlined by Mark Kinkead-Weekes.

In a reading by E. P. Shrubb, *Sons and Lovers* is seen as being about labor and its contexts, as well as about love. Paul Morel's passion returns to the center as Gavriel Ben-Ephraim emphasizes how "Paul claims therapeutic properties for sexuality that much of the novel belies." In this volume's final essay, Daniel J. Schneider shows how the novel elaborates a pattern of thwarted selfhood.

Introduction

Lawrence's *Sons and Lovers* (1913), his third novel, was begun in 1910 as *Paul Morel,* and in some sense was finished by Edward Garnett, who made severe cuts in the final manuscript. The change of title from *Paul Morel* to *Sons and Lovers* may have been Lawrence's gesture towards Freud, as mediated by Frieda Weekley, with whom Lawrence eloped in the spring of 1912 and under whose early influence the novel was completed. Lawrence attempted to fight off Freud later on, in two very odd books on the unconscious, but *Sons and Lovers* is so available to Freudian reduction as to make a Freudian reading of the novel quite uninteresting.

Though *Sons and Lovers* is clearly the work of the author of *The Rainbow* and *Women in Love,* it retains many of the characteristics of the fiction of Thomas Hardy and has little of the visionary intensity that the mature Lawrence shares with *Moby-Dick, Wuthering Heights,* and only a few other novels. Rereading *Sons and Lovers* is a somber and impressive experience, if a rather mixed one aesthetically. It is difficult to know if we are reading an autobiographical novel rather than a novelistic autobiography. The aesthetic puzzle is in deciding how to receive Lawrence's self-portrait as Paul Morel. If the reader simply decides that the identification of the writer and his hero is complete, then the experience of reading necessarily is vexed by the identification of Gertrude Morel with Lydia Lawrence, the novelist's mother, and so also by the parody of Arthur Lawrence in the novel's Walter Morel. Even more troublesome is the identification of Jessie Chambers, the novelist's first love, with Miriam. By the time one has read *D. H. Lawrence: A Personal Record* by Jessie Chambers and studied such standard biographies of Lawrence as those by Nehls, Moore, and Sagar, it becomes very difficult to know whether the novel is the appropriate genre for Lawrence's story. Miriam and Wal-

1

ter Morel seem abused in *Sons and Lovers,* and Paul Morel seems quite blind to his mother's real culpability in malforming his psychosexual development.

A curious reader or student of D. H. Lawrence will search out the appropriate material in the composite biography of Nehls, but I am dubious as to whether *Sons and Lovers* gains aesthetically by such an enrichment of personal context. Louis L. Martz has argued that a close reading will show that the novel depicts Miriam as life-enhancing and Gertrude Morel as an agent of repression, but the book's actual narrative voice tends to give an impression much closer to that of Paul, who ends by leaving Miriam and then confronting a motherless Sublime that has no place for him:

> He shook hands and left her at the door of her cousin's house. When he turned away he felt the last hold for him had gone. The town, as he sat upon the car, stretched away over the bay of railway, a level fume of lights. Beyond the town the country, little smouldering spots for more towns—the sea—the night—on and on! And he had no place in it! Whatever spot he stood on, there he stood alone. From his breast, from his mouth, sprang the endless space, and it was there behind him, everywhere. The people hurrying along the streets offered no obstruction to the void in which he found himself. They were small shadows whose footsteps and voices could be heard, but in each of them the same night, the same silence. He got off the car. In the country all was dead still. Little stars shone high up; little stars spread far away in the flood-waters, a firmament below. Everywhere the vastness and terror of the immense night which is roused and stirred for a brief while by the day, but which returns, and will remain at last eternal, holding everything in its silence and its living gloom. There was no Time, only Space. Who could say his mother had lived and did not live? She had been in one place, and was in another; that was all. And his soul could not leave her, wherever she was. Now she was gone abroad into the night, and he was with her still. They were together. But yet there was his body, his chest, that leaned against the stile, his hands on the wooden bar. They seemed something. Where was he?—one tiny upright

speck of flesh, less than an ear of wheat lost in the field. He could not bear it. On every side the immense dark silence seemed pressing him, so tiny a spark, into extinction, and yet, almost nothing, he could not be extinct. Night, in which everything was lost, went reaching out, beyond stars and sun. Stars and sun, a few bright grains, went spinning round for terror, and holding each other in embrace, there in a darkness that outpassed them all, and left them tiny and daunted. So much, and himself, infinitesimal, at the core a nothingness, and yet not nothing.

"Mother!" he whimpered—"mother!"

She was the only thing that held him up, himself, amid all this. And she was gone, intermingled herself. He wanted her to touch him, have him alongside with her.

But no, he would not give in. Turning sharply, he walked towards the city's gold phosphorescence. His fists were shut, his mouth set fast. He would not take that direction, to the darkness, to follow her. He walked towards the faintly humming, glowing town, quickly.

We understand, after reading this conclusion to *Sons and Lovers*, why Walt Whitman came to have so powerful an influence upon Lawrence's later poetry, since the elegiac Whitman identified night, death, the mother, and the sea, and only the sea is absent from the fusion here. Nothing else in *Sons and Lovers* is quite as strong as this closing vision, which does prophesy the greater harmonies and discords of *The Rainbow* and *Women in Love*.

Aside from the troublesome strains of unassimilated autobiography, the principal defect of *Sons and Lovers* is that Paul Morel does not always seem energetic or sympathetic enough to sustain our interest. At moments we might be reading *A Portrait of the Artist as a Young Prig,* and we then want to congratulate Miriam for not ending up with the hero. The novel has force of narrative despite lack of plot, and deserves all the praise it has received as an unmatched account of English working-class life. But the sincerity or veracity of Lawrence's story of his own origins is more of a social than an aesthetic virtue in *Sons and Lovers*. What redeems the book aesthetically is a series of passages and incidents that presage the massive excursions into the Sublime made in *The Rainbow* and *Women in Love*. The concluding passage is one of these; others include such famous moments as Paul and Miriam taking turns on the swing, and the fight between Paul and Baxter Dawes (who is oddly the most convincing character in the novel). These are early forms of what might be called Lawrence's epiphanies, times when elemental forces break through the surfaces of existence. Lawrence hardly knows what to do with them in *Sons and Lovers;* they do not reverberate with enormous possibilities as do such moments in *Women in Love* as Birkin stoning the moon's reflection in the water, or Birkin and Gerald caught up in their wrestling match. Yet the shadowy epiphanies of *Sons and Lovers* have the value of preparatory exercises for those fragments of a giant art that Lawrence later scattered so generously in his work.

On *Sons and Lovers*

Dorothy Van Ghent

Novels, like other dramatic art, deal with conflicts of one kind or another—conflicts that are, in the work of the major novelists, drawn from life in the sense that they are representative of real problems in life; and the usual urgency in the novelist is to find the technical means which will afford an ideal resolution of the conflict and solution of the living problem—still "ideal" even if tragic. Technique is his art itself, in its procedural aspect; and the validity of his solution of a problem is dependent upon the adequacy of his technique. The more complex and intransigent the problem, the more subtle his technical strategies will evidently need to be, if they are to be effective. The decade of World War I brought into full and terrible view the collapse of values that had prophetically haunted the minds of novelists as far back as Dostoevsky and Flaubert and Dickens, or even farther back, to Balzac and Stendhal. With that decade, and increasingly since, the problems of modern life have appeared intransigent indeed; and, in general, the growth of that intransigence has been reflected in an increasing concern with technique on the part of the artist. D. H. Lawrence's sensitivity to twentieth-century chaos was peculiarly intense, and his passion for order was similarly intense; but this sensitivity and this passion did not lead him to concentrate on refinements and subtleties of novelistic technique in the direction laid out, for instance, by James and Conrad. Hence, as

From *The English Novel: Form and Function.* © 1953 by Dorothy Van Ghent. Harper & Brothers, 1961.

readers first approaching his work, almost inevitably we feel disappointment and even perhaps shock, that writing so often "loose" and repetitious and such unrestrained emotionalism over glandular matters should appear in the work of a novelist who is assumed to have an important place in the literary canon. "There is no use," Francis Fergusson says, "trying to appreciate [Lawrence] solely as an artist; he was himself too often impatient of the demands of art, which seemed to him trivial compared with the quest he followed." And Stephen Spender phrases the problem of Lawrence in this way: what interested him "was the tension between art and life, not the complete resolution of the problems of life within the illusion of art. . . . For him literature is a kind of pointer to what is outside literature. . . . This outsideness of reality is for Lawrence the waters of baptism in which man can be reborn." We need to approach Lawrence with a good deal of humility about "art" and a good deal of patience for the disappointments he frequently offers as an artist, for it is only thus that we shall be able to appreciate the innovations he actually made in the novel as well as the importance and profundity of his vision of modern life.

Sons and Lovers appears to have the most conventional chronological organization—the extreme reverse of Conrad's intricate cross-chronology; it is the kind of organization that a naive autobiographical novelist would tend to use, with only the thinnest pretense at disguising the personally retrospective nature of the material. We start with the marriage of the parents and the birth of the children. We learn of the daily life of the family while the children are growing up, the work, the small joys, the parental strife. Certain well-defined emotional pressures become apparent: the children are alienated from their father, whose personality degenerates gradually as he feels his exclusion; the mother more and more completely dominates her sons' affections, aspirations, mental habits. Urged by her toward middle-class refinements, they enter white-collar jobs, thus making one more dissociation between themselves and their proletarian father. As they attempt to orient themselves toward biological adulthood, the old split in the family is manifested in a new form, as an internal schism in the characters of the sons; they cannot reconcile sexual choice with the idealism their mother has inculcated. This inner strain leads to the older son's death. The same motif is repeated in the case of Paul, the younger one. Paul's first girl, Miriam, is a cerebral type, and the mother senses in her an obvious rivalry for domination of Paul's sensibility. The mother is the stronger influence, and Paul withdraws from Miriam; but with her own victory Mrs. Morel begins to realize the discord she has produced in his character, and tries to release her hold on him by unconsciously seeking her own death. Paul finds another girl, Clara, but the damage is already too deeply designed, and at the time of his mother's death, he voluntarily gives up Clara, knowing that there is but one direction he can take, and that is to go with his mother. At the end he is left emotionally derelict, with only the "drift toward death."

From this slight sketch, it is clear that the book is organized not merely on a chronological plan showing the habits and vicissitudes of a Nottinghamshire miner's family, but that it has a structure rigorously controlled by an idea: an idea of an organic disturbance in the relationships of men and women—a disturbance of sexual polarities that is first seen in the disaffection of mother and father, then in the mother's attempt to substitute her sons for her husband, finally in the sons' unsuccessful struggle to establish natural manhood. Lawrence's development of the idea has certain major implications: it implies that his characters have transgressed against the natural life-directed condition of the human animal—against the elementary biological rhythms he shares with the rest of biological nature; and it implies that this offense against life has been brought about by a failure to respect the complete and terminal individuality of persons—by a twisted desire to "possess" other persons, as the mother tries to "possess" her husband, then her sons, and as Miriam tries to "possess" Paul. Lawrence saw this offense as a disease of modern life in all its manifestations, from sexual relationships to those broad social and political relationships that have changed people from individuals to anonymous economic properties or to military units or to ideological automatons.

The controlling idea is expressed in the various episodes—the narrative logic of the book. It is also expressed in imagery—the book's poetic logic. In previous studies we have discussed, from a number of points of view, the function of imagery in novels, but nowhere else do we find the image so largely replacing episode and discursive analysis and taking over the expressive functions of these, as it does in Lawrence. The chief reason for the extraordinary predominance of the image, as an absolute expressive medium, in Lawrence, lies in the character of the idea which is his subject. He must make us aware—sensitively aware, not merely conceptually aware—

of the profound life force whose rhythms the natural creature obeys; and he must make us aware of the terminal individuality—the absolute "otherness" or "outsideness"—that is the natural form of things and of the uncorrupted person. We must be made aware of these through the *feelings* of his people, for only in feeling have the biological life force and the sense of identity, either the identity of self or of others, any immediacy of reality. He seeks the objective equivalent of feeling in the image. As Francis Fergusson says, Lawrence's imagination was so concrete that he seems not "to distinguish between the reality and the metaphor or symbol which makes it plain to us." But the most valid symbols are the most concrete realities. Lawrence's great gift for the symbolic image was a function of his sensitivity to and passion for the meaning of real things—for the individual expression that real forms have. In other words, his gift for the image arose directly from his vision of life as infinitely creative of individual identities, each whole and separate and to be reverenced as such.

Let us examine the passage with which the first chapter of *Sons and Lovers* ends—where Mrs. Morel, pregnant with Paul, wanders deliriously in the garden, shut out of the house by Morel in his drunkenness. Mrs. Morel is literally a vessel of the life force that seems to thrust itself at her in nature from all sides, but she is also in rebellion against it and the perfume of the pollen-filled lilies makes her gasp with fear.

> The moon was high and magnificent in the August night. Mrs. Morel, seared with passion, shivered to find herself out there in a great white light, that fell cold on her, and gave a shock to her inflamed soul. She stood for a few moments helplessly staring at the glistening great rhubarb leaves near the door. Then she got the air into her breast. She walked down the garden path, trembling in every limb, while the child boiled within her. . . .
>
> She hurried out of the side garden to the front, where she could stand as if in an immense gulf of white light, the moon streaming high in face of her, the moonlight standing up from the hills in front, and filling the valley where the Bottoms crouched, almost blindingly. There, panting and half weeping in reaction from the stress, she murmured to herself over and over again: "The nuisance! the nuisance!"

She became aware of something about her. With an effort she roused herself to see what it was that penetrated her consciousness. The tall white lilies were reeling in the moonlight, and the air was charged with their perfume, as with a presence. Mrs. Morel gasped slightly in fear. She touched the big, pallid flowers on their petals, then shivered. They seemed to be stretching in the moonlight. She put her hand into one white bin: the gold scarcely showed on her fingers by moonlight. She bent down to look at the binful of yellow pollen; but it only appeared dusky. Then she drank a deep draught of the scent. It almost made her dizzy.

Mrs. Morel leaned on the garden gate, looking out, and she lost herself awhile. She did not know what she thought. Except for a slight feeling of sickness, and her consciousness in the child, herself melted out like a scent into the shiny, pale air.

She finally arouses Morel from his drunken sleep and he lets her in. Unfastening her brooch at the bedroom mirror, she sees that her face is smeared with the yellow dust of the lilies.

The imagery of the streaming moonlight is that of a vast torrential force, "magnificent" and inhuman, and it equates not only with that phallic power of which Mrs. Morel is the rebellious vessel but with the greater and universal demiurge that was anciently called Eros—the power springing in plants and hurling the planets, giving the "glistening great rhubarb leaves" their fierce identity, fecundating and stretching the lilies. The smear of yellow pollen on Mrs. Morel's face is a grossly humorous irony. This passage is a typifying instance of the spontaneous identification Lawrence constantly found between image and meaning, between real things and what they symbolize.

Our particular culture has evolved deep prohibitions against the expression, or even the subjective acknowledgment of the kind of phallic reality with which Lawrence was concerned—and with which ancient religions were also concerned. Certainly one factor in the uneasiness that Lawrence frequently causes us is the factor of those cultural prohibitions. But these prohibitions themselves Lawrence saw as disease symptoms, though the disease was far more extensive and radical than a taboo on the phallus. It was a spiritual disease that broke down the sense of identity, of "separate selfhood," while at the same time it broke down the sense of rhythm with universal nature. Paul Morel, working his fairly unconscious, adolescent, sexual way toward Miriam, finds that rhythm and that selfhood in the spatial proportions of a wren's nest in a hedge.

> He crouched down and carefully put his finger through the thorns into the round door of the nest.
> "It's almost as if you were feeling inside the live body of the bird," he said, "it's so warm. They say a bird makes its nest round like a cup with pressing its breast on it. Then how did it make the ceiling round, I wonder?"

When Paul takes his first country walk with Clara and Miriam, the appearance of a red stallion in the woods vividly realizes in unforced symbolic dimension the power which will drive Paul from Miriam to Clara, while the image also realizes the great horse itself in its unique and mysterious identity.

> As they were going beside the brook, on the Willey Water side, looking through the brake at the edge of the wood, where pink campions glowed under a few sunbeams, they saw, beyond the tree-trunks and the thin hazel bushes, a man leading a great bay horse through the gullies. The big red beast seemed to dance romantically through that dimness of green hazel drift, away there where the air was shadowy, as if it were in the past, among the fading bluebells that might have bloomed for Deirdre. . . .
> The great horse breathed heavily, shifting round its red flanks, and looking suspiciously with its wonderful big eyes upwards from under its lowered head and falling mane.

A simple descriptive passage like the following, showing a hen pecking at a girl's hand, conveys the animal dynamics that is the urgent phase of the phallic power working in the boy and the girl, but its spontaneous symbolism of a larger reality is due to its faithfulness to the way a hen does peck and the feeling of the pecking—due, that is, to the actuality or "identity" of the small, homely circumstance itself.

> As he went round the back, he saw Miriam kneeling in front of the hen-coop, some maize in her hand, biting her

lip, and crouching in an intense attitude. The hen was eye-
ing her wickedly. Very gingerly she put forward her hand.
The hen bobbed for her. She drew back quickly with a cry,
half of fear, half of chagrin.

"It won't hurt you," said Paul.

She flushed crimson and started up.

"I only wanted to try," she said in a low voice.

"See, it doesn't hurt," he said, and, putting only two
corns in his palm, he let the hen peck, peck, peck at his
bare hand. "It only makes you laugh," he said.

She put her hand forward, and dragged it away, tried
again, and started back with a cry. He frowned.

"Why, I'd let her take corn from my face," said Paul,
"only she bumps a bit. She's ever so neat. If she wasn't,
look how much ground she'd peck up every day."

He waited grimly, and watched. At last Miriam let the
bird peck from her hand. She gave a little cry—fear, and
pain because of fear—rather pathetic. But she had done it,
and she did it again.

"There, you see," said the boy. "It doesn't hurt, does it?"

There is more terse and obvious symbolism, of the typical kind in
Lawrence, in that sequence where Clara's red carnations splatter their
petals over her clothes and on the ground where she and Paul first
make love, but we acquire the best and the controlling sense of Lawrence's gift for the image, as dramatic and thematic expression, in
those passages where his urgency is to see *things* and to see them
clearly and completely in their most individualizing traits, for the
character of his vision is such that, in truly seeing them as they are,
he sees through them to what they mean.

We have fairly frequently noticed in these studies the differen-
tiating significance of a writer's treatment of nature—that is, of that
part of "nature" which is constituted by earth and air and water and
the nonhuman creatures; and we have found that attitudes toward
nature were deeply associated with attitudes toward human "good,"
human destiny, human happiness, human salvation, the characteristic problems of being human. One might cite, for instance, in *Tom
Jones,* Fielding's highly stylized treatment of outdoor nature (as in
the passage in which Tom dreams of Sophia beside the brook, and
Mollie Seagrim approaches): here nature has only generalized attri-

butes for whose description and understanding certain epithets in common educated currency are completely adequate—brooks murmur, breezes whisper, birds trill; nature is really a linguistic construction, and this rationalization of nature is appropriate in Fielding's universe since everything there exists ideally as an object of *ratio,* of reasoning intelligence. We have noticed in Jane Austen's *Pride and Prejudice* (in the description of Darcy's estate, for example) that outdoor nature again has importance only as it serves to express rational and social character—wherefore again the generalized epithet that represents nature as either the servant of intelligence or the space where intelligence operates. In George Eliot's *Adam Bede,* where there is relatively a great deal of "outdoors," nature is man's plowfield, the acre in which he finds social and ethical expression through work; this is only a different variety of the conception of nature as significant by virtue of what man's intelligential and social character makes of it for his ends.

With Emily Brontë, we come nearer to Lawrence, though not very near. In *Wuthering Heights,* nature's importance is due not to its yielding itself up to domestication in man's reason, or offering itself as an instrument by which he expresses his conscience before God or society, but to its fiercely unregenerate difference from all that civilized man is—a difference that it constantly forces on perception by animal-like attacks on and disruptions of human order. In Hardy, nature is also a daemonic entity in its own right, and not only unrationalizable but specifically hostile to the human reason. It is worth noting that, among all English novelists, Hardy and Lawrence have the most faithful touch for the things of nature and the greatest evocative genius in bringing them before the imagination. But there are certain definitive differences of attitude. Both Emily Brontë's and Hardy's worlds are dual, and there is no way of bringing the oppositions of the dualism together: on the one side of the cleavage are those attributes of man that we call "human," his reason, his ethical sensibility; and on the other side is "nature"—the elements and the creatures and man's own instinctive life that he shares with the nonhuman creatures. The opposition is resolved only by destruction of the "human": a destruction that is in Emily Brontë profoundly attractive, in Hardy tragic. But Lawrence's world is multiple rather than dual. Everything in it is a separate and individual "other," every person, every creature, every object (like the madonna lilies, the rhubarb plants, the wren's nest, the stallion); and there is a creative relationship between people and between people and things so long as this "otherness" is acknowledged. When it is denied—and it is denied when man tries to rationalize nature and society, or when he presumptuously assumes the things of nature to be merely instruments for the expression of himself, or when he attempts to exercise personal possessorship over people—then he destroys his own selfhood and exerts a destructive influence all about him.

In *Sons and Lovers,* only in Morel himself, brutalized and spiritually maimed as he is, does the germ of selfhood remain intact; and—this is the correlative proposition in Lawrence—in him only does the biological life force have simple, unequivocal assertion. Morel wants to live, by hook or crook, while his sons want to die. To live is to obey a rhythm involving more than conscious attitudes and involving more than human beings—involving all nature; a rhythm indifferent to the greediness of reason, indifferent to idiosyncrasies of culture and idealism. The image associated with Morel is that of the coalpits, where he descends daily and from which he ascends at night blackened and tired. It is a symbol of rhythmic descent and ascent, like a sexual rhythm, or like the rhythm of sleep and awaking or of death and life. True, the work in the coalpits reverses the natural use of the hours of light and dark and is an economic distortion of that rhythm in nature—and Morel and the other colliers bear the spiritual traumata of that distortion; for Lawrence is dealing with the real environment of modern men, in its complexity and injuriousness. Nevertheless, the work at the pits is still symbolic of the greater rhythm governing life and obedience to which is salvation. Throughout the book, the coalpits are always at the horizon.

> On the fallow land the young wheat shone silkily. Minton pit waved its plumes of white steam, coughed, and rattled hoarsely.
>
> "Now look at that!" said Mrs. Morel. Mother and son stood on the road to watch. Along the ridge of the great pit-hill crawled a little group in silhouette against the sky, a horse, a small truck, and a man. They climbed the incline against the heavens. At the end the man tipped the waggon. There was an undue rattle as the waste fell down the sheer slope of the enormous bank. . . .
>
> "Look how it heaps together," [Paul says of the pit] "like something alive almost—a big creature that you don't

know. . . . And all the trucks standing waiting, like a
string of beasts to be fed. . . . I like the feel of *men* on
things, while they're alive. There's a feel of men about
trucks, because they've been handled with men's hands, all
of them."

Paul associates the pits not only with virility but with being alive.
The trucks themselves become alive because they have been handled
by men. The symbolism of the pits is identical with that of Morel,
the father, the irrational life principle that is unequally embattled
against the death principle in the mother, the rational and idealiz-
ing principle working rhythmlessly, greedily, presumptuously, and
possessively.

The sons' attitude toward the father is ambivalent, weighted toward hate because the superior cultural equipment of the mother
shows his crudeness in relief; but again and again bits of homely
characterization of Morel show that the children—and even the
mother herself—sense, however uncomfortably, the attractiveness of
his simple masculine integrity. He has, uninjurable, what the mother's possessiveness has injured in the sons.

> "Shut that doo-er!" bawled Morel furiously.
> Annie banged it behind her, and was gone.
> "If tha oppens it again while I'm weshin' me, I'll ma'e
> thy jaw rattle," he threatened from the midst of his soap-
> suds. Paul and the mother frowned to hear him.
> Presently he came running out of the scullery, with the
> soapy water dripping from him, dithering with cold.
> "Oh, my sirs!" he said. "Wheer's my towel?"
> It was hung on a chair to warm before the fire, other-
> wise he would have bullied and blustered. He squatted on
> his heels before the hot baking-fire to dry himself.
> "F-ff-f!" he went, pretending to shudder with cold.
> "Goodness, man, don't be such a kid!" said Mrs. Morel.
> "It's *not* cold."
> "Thee strip thysen stark nak'd to wesh thy flesh i' that
> scullery," said the miner, as he rubbed his hair; "nowt b'r
> a ice-'ouse!"
> "And I shouldn't make that fuss," replied his wife.
> "No, tha'd drop down stiff, as dead as a door-knob, wi'
> thy nesh sides."

"Why is a door-knob deader than anything else?" asked Paul, curious.

"Eh, I dunno; that's what they say," replied his father. "But there's that much draught i' yon scullery, as it blows through your ribs like through a five-barred gate."

"It would have some difficulty in blowing through yours," said Mrs. Morel.

Morel looked down ruefully at his sides.

"Me!" he exclaimed. "I'm nowt b'r a skinned rabbit. My bones fair juts out on me."

"I should like to know where," retorted his wife.

"Iv'ry-wheer! I'm nobbut a sack o' faggots."

Mrs. Morel laughed. He had still a wonderfully young body, muscular, without any fat. His skin was smooth and clear. It might have been the body of a man of twenty-eight, except that there were, perhaps, too many blue scars, like tattoo-marks, where the coal-dust remained under the skin, and that his chest was too hairy. But he put his hands on his sides ruefully. It was his fixed belief that, because he did not get fat, he was as thin as a starved rat.

Paul looked at his father's thick, brownish hands all scarred, with broken nails, rubbing the fine smoothness of his sides, and the incongruity struck him. It seemed strange they were the same flesh.

Morel talks the dialect that is the speech of physical tenderness in Lawrence's books. It is to the dialect of his father that Paul reverts when he is tussling with Beatrice in adolescent erotic play (letting the mother's bread burn, that he should have been watching), and that Arthur, the only one of the sons whom the mother has not corrupted, uses in his lovemaking, and that Paul uses again when he makes love to Clara, the uncomplex woman who is able for a while to give him his sexual manhood and his "separate selfhood." The sons never use the dialect with their mother, and Paul never uses it with Miriam. It is the speech used by Mellors in *Lady Chatterley's Lover;* and, significantly perhaps, Mellors's name is an anagram on the name Morel.

Some of the best moments in the children's life are associated with the father, when Morel has his "good" periods and enters again into the intimate activity of the family—and some of the best, most simply objective writing in the book communicates these moments, as for instance the passage in chapter 4 where Morel is engaged in making fuses.

> Morel fetched a sheaf of long sound wheat-straws from the attic. These he cleaned with his hand, till each one gleamed like a stalk of gold, after which he cut the straws into lengths of about six inches, leaving, if he could, a notch at the bottom of each piece. He always had a beautifully sharp knife that could cut a straw clean without hurting it. Then he set in the middle of the table a heap of gun-powder, a little pile of black grains upon the white-scrubbed board. He made and trimmed the straws while Paul and Annie filled and plugged them. Paul loved to see the black grains trickle down a crack in his palm into the mouth of the straw, peppering jollily downwards till the straw was full. Then he bunged up the mouth with a bit of soap—which he got on his thumb-nail from a pat in a saucer—and the straw was finished.

There is a purity of realization in this very simple kind of exposition that, on the face of it, resists associating itself with any *symbolic* function—if we tend to think of a "symbol" as splitting itself apart into a thing and a meaning, with a mental arrow connecting the two. The best in Lawrence carries the authenticity of a faithfully observed, concrete actuality that refuses to be so split; its symbolism is a radiation that leaves it intact in itself. So, in the passage above, the scene is intact as homely realism, but it radiates Lawrence's controlling sense of the characterful integrity of objects—the clean wheat straws, the whitely scrubbed table, the black grains peppering down a crack in the child's palm, the bung of soap on a thumbnail—and that integrity is here associated with the man Morel and his own integrity of warm and absolute maleness. Thus it is another representation of the creative life force witnessed in the independent objectivity of things that are wholly concrete and wholly themselves.

The human attempt to distort and corrupt that selfhood is reflected in Miriam's attitude toward flowers.

> Round the wild, tussocky lawn at the back of the house was a thorn hedge, under which daffodils were craning forward from among their sheaves of grey-green blades.

The cheeks of the flowers were greenish with cold. But still some had burst, and their gold ruffled and glowed. Miriam went on her knees before one cluster, took a wild-looking daffodil between her hands, turned up its face of gold to her, and bowed down, caressing it with her mouth and cheeks and brow. He stood aside, with his hands in his pockets, watching her. One after another she turned up to him the faces of the yellow, bursten flowers appealingly, fondling them lavishly all the while. . . .

"Why must you always be fondling things!" he said irritably. . . . "Can you never like things without clutching them as if you wanted to pull the heart out of them? . . . You're always begging things to love you. . . . Even the flowers, you have to fawn on them—"

Rhythmically, Miriam was swaying and stroking the flower with her mouth. . . .

"You don't want to love—your eternal and abnormal craving is to be loved. You aren't positive, you're negative. You absorb, absorb, as if you must fill yourself up with love, because you've got a shortage somewhere."

The relationship of the girl to the flowers is that of a blasphemous possessorship which denies the separateness of living entities—the craving to break down boundaries between thing and thing, that is seen also in Miriam's relationship with Paul, whom she cannot love without trying to absorb him. In contrast, there is the flower imagery in the eleventh chapter, where Paul goes out into the night and the garden in a moment of emotional struggle.

It grew late. Through the open door, stealthily, came the scent of madonna lilies, almost as if it were prowling abroad. Suddenly he got up and went out of doors.

The beauty of the night made him want to shout. A half-moon, dusky gold, was sinking behind the black sycamore at the end of the garden, making the sky dull purple with its glow. Nearer, a dim white fence of lilies went across the garden, and the air all round seemed to stir with scent, as if it were alive. He went across the bed of pinks, whose keen perfume came sharply across the rocking, heavy scent of the lilies, and stood alongside the white barrier of flowers. They flagged all loose, as if they were pant-

ing. The scent made him drunk. He went down to the
field to watch the moon sink under.

A corncrake in the hay-close called insistently. The
moon slid quite quickly downwards, growing more
flushed. Behind him the great flowers leaned as if they
were calling. And then, like a shock, he caught another
perfume, something raw and coarse. Hunting round, he
found the purple iris, touched their fleshy throats and their
dark, grasping hands. At any rate, he had found something. They stood stiff in the darkness. Their scent was
brutal. The moon was melting down upon the crest of the
hill. It was gone; all was dark. The corncrake called still.

The flowers here have a fierce "thereness" or "otherness" establishing
them as existences in their own right, as separate, strange selves, and
the demiurgic Eros is rudely insistent in their scent. Paul's perception
of that independent life puts him into relation with himself, and the
moment of catalytic action is marked by the brief sentence: "At any
rate, he had found something." The "something" that he finds is
simply the iris, dark, fleshy, mysterious, alien. He goes back into the
house and tells his mother that he has decided to break off with
Miriam.

Darkness—as the darkness of this night in the garden—has in
Lawrence a special symbolic potency. It is a natural and universal
symbol, but it offers itself with special richness to Lawrence because
of the character of his governing vision. Darkness is half of the
rhythm of the day, the darkness of unconsciousness is half of the
rhythm of the mind, and the darkness of death is half of the rhythm
of life. Denial of this phase of the universal tide is the great sin, the
sin committed by modern economy and modern rationalism. In acceptance of the dark, man is renewed to himself—and to light, to
consciousness, to reason, to brotherhood. But by refusal to accept
that half of the rhythm, he becomes impotent, his reason becomes
destructive, and he loses the sense of the independence of others
which is essential to brotherhood. In the thirteenth chapter of *Sons
and Lovers* there is a passage that realizes something of what we have
been saying. It occurs just after Paul has made love to Clara in a field.

All the while the peewits were screaming in the field.
When he came to, he wondered what was near his eyes,
curving and strong with life in the dark, and what voice it

was speaking. Then he realized it was the grass, and the peewit was calling. The warmth was Clara's breathing heaving. He lifted his head, and looked into her eyes. They were dark and shining and strange, life wild at the source staring into his life, stranger to him, yet meeting him; and he put his face down on her throat, afraid. What was she? A strong, strange, wild life, that breathed with his in the darkness through this hour. It was all so much bigger than themselves that he was hushed. They had met, and included in their meeting the thrust of the manifold grass-stems, the cry of the peewit, the wheel of the stars. . . .

After such an evening they both were very still. . . . They felt small, half afraid, childish, and wondering, like Adam and Eve when they lost their innocence and realized the magnificence of the power which drove them out of Paradise and across the great night and the great day of humanity. It was for each of them an initiation. . . . To know their own nothingness, to know the tremendous living flood which carried them always, gave them rest within themselves. If so great a magnificent power could overwhelm them, identify them altogether with itself, so that they knew they were only grains in the tremendous heave that lifted every grass-blade its little height, and every tree, and living thing, then why fret about themselves? They could let themselves be carried by life, and they felt a sort of peace each in the other. There was a verification which they had had together. Nothing could nullify it, nothing could take it away; it was almost their belief in life.

But then we are told that "Clara was not satisfied. . . . She thought it was he whom she wanted. . . . She had not got him; she was not satisfied." This is the impulse toward personal possessorship that constantly confuses and distorts human relationships in Lawrence's books; it is a denial of the otherness of people, and a denial, really, of the great inhuman life force, the primal Otherness through which people have their independent definition as well as their creative community. Paul had felt that "his experience had been impersonal, and not Clara"; and he had wanted the same impersonality in Clara, an impersonality consonant with that of the manifold grass stems and the peewits' calling and the wheel of the stars. André Malraux, in his preface to the French translation of *Lady Chatterley's Lover,* says that this "couple-advocate," Lawrence, is concerned not with his own individuality or that of his mate, but with "being": "Lawrence has no wish to be either happy or great," Malraux says; "he is only concerned with being." The concern with being, with simple being-a-self (as distinguished from imposing the ego or abdicating selfhood in the mass), can be understood only in the context of twentieth-century man's resignation to herd ideologies, herd recreations, herd rationalizations. Lawrence's missionary and prophetic impulse, like Dostoevsky's, was to combat the excesses of rationalism and individualism, excesses that have led—paradoxically enough—to the release of monstrously destructive irrationals and to the impotence of the individual. He wanted to bring man's self-definition and creativity back into existence through recognition of and vital relationship with the rhythms that men share with the nonhuman world; for he thought that thus men could find not only the selves that they had denied, but also the brotherhood they had lost.

The darkness of the phallic consciousness is the correlative of a passionate life assertion, strong as the thrust of the grass stems in the field where Paul and Clara make love, and as the dynamics of the wheeling stars. "In the lowest trough of the night" there is always "a flare of the pit." A pillar of cloud by day, the pit is a pillar of fire by night: and the Lord is at the pit top. As a descent of darkness and an ascent of flame is associated with the secret, essential, scatheless maleness of the father, so also the passionate self-forgetful play of the children is associated with a fiery light in the night—an isolated lamppost, a blood-red moon, and behind, "the great scoop of darkness, as if all the night were there." It is this understanding of the symbolism of darkness in Lawrence that gives tragic dignity to such a scene as that of the bringing home of William's coffin through the darkness of the night.

> Morel and Paul went, with a candle, into the parlour. There was no gas there. The father unscrewed the top of the big mahogany oval table, and cleared the middle of the room; then he arranged six chairs opposite each other, so that the coffin could stand on their beds.
>
> "You niver seed such a length as he is!" said the miner, and watching anxiously as he worked.

Paul went to the bay window and looked out. The ash-tree stood monstrous and black in front of the wide darkness. It was a faintly luminous night. Paul went back to his mother.

At ten o'clock Morel called:

"He's here!"

Everyone started. There was a noise of unbarring and unlocking the front door, which opened straight from the night into the room.

"Bring another candle," called Morel. . . .

There was the noise of wheels. Outside in the darkness of the street below Paul could see horses and a black vehicle, one lamp, and a few pale faces; then some men, miners, all in their shirt-sleeves, seemed to struggle in the obscurity. Presently two men appeared, bowed beneath a great weight. It was Morel and his neighbour.

"Steady!" called Morel, out of breath.

He and his fellow mounted the steep garden step, heaved into the candle-light with their gleaming coffin-end. Limbs of other men were seen struggling behind. Morel and Burns, in front, staggered; the great dark weight swayed.

"Steady, steady!" cried Morel, as if in pain. . . .

The coffin swayed, the men began to mount the three steps with their load. Annie's candle flickered, and she whimpered as the first men appeared, and the limbs and bowed heads of six men struggled to climb into the room, bearing the coffin that rode like sorrow on their living flesh.

Here the darkness appears in another indivisible aspect of its mystery—as the darkness of death. Perhaps no other modern writer besides Rilke and Mann has tried so sincerely to bring death into relationship with life as Lawrence did, and each under the assumption that life, to know itself creatively, must know its relationship with death; a relationship which the ethos of some hundred and fifty years of rationalism and industrialism and "progress" have striven to exorcise, and by that perversion brought men to an abject worship of death and to holocausts such as that of Hiroshima. *Sons and Lovers* ends with Paul a derelict in the "drift toward death," which Lawrence thought of as the disease-syndrome of his time and of Europe. But the death drift, the death worship, is for Lawrence a hideous distortion of the relationship of death to life. In the scene in which William's coffin is brought home, the front door "opened straight from the night into the room." So, in their rhythmic proportions, life and death open straight into each other, as do the light of consciousness and the darkness of the unconscious, and the usurpation of either one is a perversion of the other. Stephen Spender calls Lawrence "the most hopeful modern writer." His "dark gods," Spender says,

> are symbols of an inescapable mystery: the point of comprehension where the senses are aware of an otherness in objects which extends beyond the senses, and the possibility of a relationship between the human individual and the forces outside himself, which is capable of creating in him a new state of mind. Lawrence is the most hopeful modern writer, because he looks beyond the human to the nonhuman, which can be discovered within the human.

The Son and the Artist

H. M. Daleski

> A [Ceylonese] workman was arranging a screen on the verandah where we were seated. He was alert; with sure, graceful movement and fine head; his dark eyes flashing; his features regular; the beard clipped in an elegant line. Lawrence pensively watched him, announcing that he resembled his father—the same clean-cut and exuberant spirit, a true pagan. He added that he had not done justice to his father in *Sons and Lovers,* and felt like rewriting it. When children they had accepted the dictum of their mother that their father was a drunkard, therefore was contemptible, but that as Lawrence had grown older he had come to see him in a different light; to see his unquenchable fire and relish for living. Now [i.e., in 1922] he blamed his mother for her self-righteousness, her invulnerable Christian virtue within which she was entrenched. She had brought down terrible scenes of vituperation upon their heads from which she might have protected them.
>
> (Earl and Achsah Brewster, *D. H. Lawrence: Reminiscences and Correspondence*)

If we object that *Sons and Lovers,* though avowedly an autobiographical novel, has a validity which is independent of the real life

From *The Forked Flame: A Study of D. H. Lawrence.* © 1965 by H. M. Daleski. Northwestern University Press, 1965.

on which it is based, we are nevertheless aware that Lawrence's reservations do point to a weakness in the book. Justice is not done to "the early married life of the Morels." In effect, however, the weakness is only marginal. The weight of hostile comment which Lawrence directs against Morel is balanced by the unconscious sympathy with which he is presented dramatically, while the overt celebration of Mrs Morel is challenged by the harshness of the character in action. The artist, it would seem, penetrated to the truth which the son subsequently thought he had not seen, for the impression which Mr and Mrs Morel in fact make is not notably different from that which Lawrence had of his father and mother in later life.

Lawrence's conscious attitude to Mr and Mrs Morel is typified by the extreme statements he makes about them. We are told that Mrs Morel, for instance, "was one of those naturally exquisite people who can walk in mud without dirtying their shoes," but Morel is said to be "an outsider. He had denied the God in him." That Lawrence was of the Devil's party without knowing it, however, is suggested by the effect of one of the early scenes between the Morels:

At half-past eleven her husband came. His cheeks were very red and very shiny above his black moustache. His head nodded slightly. He was pleased with himself.

"Oh! Oh! waitin' for me, lass? I've bin 'elpin' Anthony, an' what's think he's gen me? Nowt b'r a lousy hae'f-crown, an' that's ivry penny—"

"He thinks you've made the rest up in beer," she said shortly.

"An' I 'aven't—that I 'aven't. You b'lieve me, I've 'ad very little this day, I have an' all." His voice went tender. "Here, an' I browt thee a bit o' brandysnap, an' a coconut for th' children." He laid the gingerbread and the coconut, a hairy object, on the table. "Nay, tha niver said thankyer for nowt i' thy life, did ter?"

As a compromise, she picked up the coconut and shook it, to see if it had any milk.

"It's a good 'un, you may back yer life o' that. I got it fra' Bill Hodgkisson. 'Bill,' I says, 'tha non wants them three nuts, does ter? Arena ter for gi'ein' me one for my bit of a lad an' wench?' 'I ham, Walter, my lad,' 'e says; 'ta'e which on 'em ter's a mind.' An' so I took one, an' thanked 'im. I didn't like ter shake it afore 'is eyes, but 'e says, 'Tha'd better ma'e sure it's a good un, Walt.' An' so, yer see, I knowed it was. He's a nice chap, is Bill Hodgkisson, 'e's a nice chap!"

"A man will part with anything so long as he's drunk, and you're drunk along with him," said Mrs Morel.

"Eh, tha mucky little 'ussy, who's drunk, I sh'd like ter know?" said Morel. He was extraordinarily pleased with himself, because of his day's helping to wait in the Moon and Stars. He chattered on.

Mrs Morel, very tired, and sick of his babble, went to bed as quickly as possible, while he raked the fire.

The difference between the Morels is epitomized in the way they react to the gift of the coconut. Despite his roughness, Morel has a natural delicacy which prevents him from shaking the coconut in front of Bill Hodgkisson, though he is tempted to do so; but Mrs Morel, who usually regulates her conduct according to standards of formal propriety, is unfailingly graceless to her husband. Her shaking of the coconut, moreover, exemplifies her hard, cold materialism which makes her view the miner's drinking as a financial, as well as a moral, tragedy. At the same time—and it is this rich comprehensiveness which distinguishes Lawrence's writing in *Sons and Lovers*—her querulousness is provoked by her husband's having left her to her own devices on the day of the wakes. In the clash of temperament which explodes in the violent quarrels to which this scene is a prelude there is justification on both sides.

The scene is also representative in a way apparently not realized by Lawrence: Morel's warmth and exuberance emerge plainly from it, and there is in it more than a hint of Mrs Morel's martyred self-righteousness. This view of the Morels corresponds to that given of Lawrence's parents in *A Collier's Friday Night,* the posthumous play which preceded *Sons and Lovers* by several years, and in "Adolf" and "Rex," two sketches roughly contemporaneous with the novel. What differentiates the presentation of the Morels from that of the parents in the other work, however, is the author's interpolative antagonism in *Sons and Lovers* towards the father. In "Rex," for example, the father is said to have an "amiable but to us heartless voice" when he shouts at the children's newly acquired pet. The phrase is clumsy but it makes an effectively moderating qualification.

Such qualifications, where they are to be found in *Sons and Lovers,* are speedily offset by fierce damning. Lawrence's attitude to Morel is indeed close to that which Blake believed Milton held towards Satan; both writers are not only unconsciously sympathetic to the hated figures but hasten to correct explicitly any unfortunately favourable impressions which the characters may make:

> Both [William and Annie] hushed into silence as they heard the approaching thud of their father's stockinged feet, and shrank as he entered. Yet he was usually indulgent to them.
>
> Morel made the meal alone, brutally. He ate and drank more noisily than he had need. No one spoke to him. The family life withdrew, shrank away, and became hushed as he entered. But he cared no longer about his alienation.
>
> Immediately he had finished tea he rose with alacrity to go out. It was this alacrity, this haste to be gone, which so sickened Mrs Morel. As she heard him sousing heartily in cold water, heard the eager scratch of the steel comb on the side of the bowl, as he wetted his hair, she closed her eyes in disgust. As he bent over, lacing his boots, there was a certain vulgar gusto in his movement that divided him from the reserved, watchful rest of the family. He always ran away from the battle with himself. Even in his own heart's privacy, he excused himself, saying, "If she hadn't said so-and-so, it would never have happened. She asked for what she's got." The children waited in restraint during his preparations. When he had gone, they sighed with relief.
>
> He closed the door behind him, and was glad. It was a rainy evening. The Palmerston would be the cosier. . . .
>
> "What shollt ha'e, Walter?" cried a voice, as soon as Morel appeared in the doorway.
>
> "Oh, Jim, my lad, wheriver has thee sprung frae?"
>
> The men made a seat for him, and took him in warmly. He was glad. In a minute or two they had thawed all responsibility out of him, all shame, all trouble, and he was clear as a bell for a jolly night.

This passage is a clear example of the battle which the son wages against the artist in the early part of the book. Indeed the divergence between the two views provided of Morel is so great that the passage is subject to mutually contradictory readings. On the one hand, once the token qualification is made by the allusion to Morel's usual indulgence to the children, the eye that sees him is consistently hostile. He eats "brutally" and his natural gusto is "vulgar"; then he ignominiously runs away from the battle with himself, taking refuge in drink. The description might have a certain validity—for it refers to Morel's behaviour after one of the worst incidents between him and his wife which culminates in his throwing a drawer at her—were it not for the fact that the eye that hardens on Morel sees the rest of the scene so clearly. As a result we see that Morel *does* care about his alienation and that his brutal eating is in fact a protest against it; that his gusto is only vulgar because it is not shared by "the reserved, watchful rest of the family"; that he runs away not so much from himself as from his wife's disgust and his children's shrinking; and that what the warmth of the Palmerston "thaws" out of him (the word is significant) is as much the icy disdain of his family as "all responsibility . . . all shame, all trouble."

It is, therefore, Lawrence's interpretative commentary on the relationship of the Morels that fails; his dramatic presentation of them never falters. The high quality of the dramatic achievement is evident, for instance, in the description of the Morels' quarrel which precedes the passage just quoted:

> He leaned on the table with one hand, and with the other jerked at the table drawer to get a knife to cut bread. The drawer stuck because he pulled sideways. In a temper he dragged it, so that it flew out bodily, and spoons, forks, knives, a hundred metallic things, splashed with a clatter and a clang upon the brick floor. The baby gave a little convulsed start.
>
> "What are you doing, clumsy, drunken fool?" the mother cried.
>
> "Then tha should get the flamin' thing thysen. Tha should get up, like other women have to, an' wait on a man."
>
> "Wait on you—wait on you?" she cried. "Yes, I see myself."
>
> "Yis, an' I'll learn thee tha's got to. Wait on *me,* yes, tha sh'lt wait on me—"

> "Never, milord. I'd wait on a dog at the door first."
> "What—what?"
>
> He was trying to fit in the drawer. At her last speech he turned round. His face was crimson, his eyes bloodshot. He stared at her one silent second in threat.
>
> "P-h!" she went quickly, in contempt.
>
> He jerked at the drawer in his excitement. It fell, cut sharply on his shin, and on the reflex he flung it at her.

In this passage the subtle complexity of life itself is rendered with a rich immediacy. The class difference between the Morels, which manifests itself here in the altercation over the duties of a working-class woman, is only a facet of their temperamental hostility. The hostility is there, lying dormant but charged, and like a booby trap it is ready to explode at the slightest touch. The explosion, when it comes, is timed to a nicety. It is the convulsed start of the baby in her arms as well as the clatter of the dropped cutlery that rouses Mrs Morel. Forgetting her earlier resolution to "say nothing" to her husband "whatever time he comes," she releases her pent-up envy and irritation in a venomous scorn which Morel cannot hope to match other than by arrogantly asserting his rights. And it is as much her final "p-h" of contempt as the reflex reaction to pain that makes him fling the drawer at her. Morel is of course factually responsible for the attack on his wife, but it is forcefully suggested that moral responsibility for the clash is Mrs Morel's; it is she who goads him into fury. Yet in the scene in which Morel takes himself off to the Palmerston it is implied that blame for the incident attaches to him alone. It is very much as if Lawrence shirks the conclusions of his own art.

Lawrence is equivocal too in his apportionment of blame for the failure of the marriage as a whole:

> Paul looked at his father's thick, brownish hands all scarred, with broken nails, rubbing the fine smoothness of his sides, and the incongruity struck him. It seemed strange they were the same flesh.
>
> "I suppose," he said to his father, "you had a good figure once."
>
> "Eh!" exclaimed the miner, glancing round, startled and timid, like a child.
>
> "He had," exclaimed Mrs Morel, "if he didn't hurtle

himself up as if he was trying to get in the smallest space he could."

"Me!" exclaimed Morel—"me a good figure! I wor niver much more n'r a skeleton."

"Man!" cried his wife, "don't be such a pulamiter!"

" 'Strewth!" he said. "Tha's niver knowed me but what I looked as if I wor goin' off in a rapid decline."

She sat and laughed.

"You've had a constitution like iron," she said, "and never a man had a better start, if it was body that counted. You should have seen him as a young man," she cried suddenly to Paul, drawing herself up to imitate her husband's once handsome bearing.

Morel watched her shyly. He saw again the passion she had had for him. It blazed upon her for a moment. He was shy, rather scared, and humble. Yet again he felt his old glow. And then immediately he felt the ruin he had made during these years.

What the book plainly shows, time and again, is that the Morels are—at the least—equally responsible for the failure of their marriage; and yet Morel is here presented as feeling that the ruin is of his making. Indeed, if ultimate responsibility for the ruin must be fixed, then on the objective evidence offered by the book it is Mrs Morel who has the most to answer for. The moment of rare marital harmony depicted in the passage illuminates the nature of her responsibility. Body counts for more than she realizes, and through failing to make the most of Morel's physical glow, she has forfeited not only the lovable husband that he is here shown to be but her own transfiguring blaze of passion, which for a moment lights her up in middle age. Earlier in the book Paul sees his mother looking "brave and rich with life, but as if she had been done out of her rights. It hurt the boy keenly, this feeling about her that she had never had her life's fulfilment": it is she who has done herself out of her rights, and it is a mark of Lawrence's ambivalent handling of the Morels that he is fully aware of this:

She still had her high moral sense, inherited from generations of Puritans. It was now a religious instinct, and she was almost a fanatic with him, because she loved him, or had loved him. If he sinned, she tortured him. If he drank, and lied, was often a poltroon, sometimes a knave, she wielded the lash unmercifully.

The pity was, she was too much his opposite. She could not be content with the little he might be; she would have him the much that he ought to be. So, in seeking to make him nobler than he could be, she destroyed him. She injured and hurt and scarred herself, but she lost none of her worth. She also had the children.

"Tortured" and "destroyed" are strong words, and "but she lost none of her worth" is an equivocal reservation. It is clear what Mrs Morel has lost, and it is to make up for it that she turns possessively, and as relentlessly as she ruined her husband, to her sons.

II

Lawrence's portrayal of Paul's relations with his father and mother has none of the distortion which weakens his representation of the marriage. To the extent that he is to be identified with Paul, he made it clear that the portrayal, among other things, was a deliberate self-purgation: "I felt you had gone off from me a bit, because of *Sons and Lovers,*" he wrote to a friend. "But one sheds one's sicknesses in books—repeats and presents again one's emotions, to be master of them." From the outset he has a clear understanding of the nature of Paul's love for his mother and his hatred of his father.

Paul is early overwhelmed by the unnatural love which his mother fosters in him. When he is a young boy she accepts the flowers which he brings her like "a woman accepting a love-token"; on the day that he goes for his interview at Jordan's she is gay with him, "like a sweetheart," and they walk through the streets of Nottingham "feeling the excitement of lovers having an adventure together"; and, eventually, everything he does is "for her"—"the two shared lives." As far as Paul's relations with his father are concerned, the boy is from infancy united with his mother against him. When Morel cuts his wife's forehead open with the drawer which he flings at her, it is Paul whom she is holding on her lap, and as she averts her face from Morel's stumbling concern, blood from the wound drips on to the baby's hair; Morel is sure that it soaks through to the scalp. This additional, if symbolic, tie of blood which Paul shares with his mother in her withdrawal from Morel is set over and against his more matter-of-fact connection with his father. As he grows up Paul is convinced of his hatred for his father:

> Paul hated his father. As a boy he had a fervent private religion.
>
> "Make him stop drinking," he prayed every night. "Lord, let my father die," he prayed very often. "Let him not be killed at pit," he prayed when, after tea, the father did not come home from work.

This is a delightful example of childish inconsequence; it is also, despite the initial affirmation, indicative of Paul's ambivalence towards his father.

That Lawrence knows what is behind Paul's excessive feelings of love and hate is asserted by one of the subtlest scenes in the book:

> He had taken off his collar and tie, and rose, bare-throated, to go to bed. As he stooped to kiss his mother, she threw her arms round his neck, hid her face on his shoulder, and cried, in a whimpering voice, so unlike her own that he writhed in agony:
>
> "I can't bear it. I could let another woman—but not her. She'd leave me no room, not a bit of room—"
>
> And immediately he hated Miriam bitterly.
>
> "And I've never—you know, Paul—I've never had a husband—not really—"
>
> He stroked his mother's hair, and his mouth was on her throat.
>
> "And she exults so in taking you from me—she's not like ordinary girls."
>
> "Well, I don't love her, Mother," he murmured, bowing his head and hiding his eyes on her shoulder in misery. His mother kissed him a long, fervent kiss.
>
> "My boy!" she said, in a voice trembling with passionate love.
>
> Without knowing, he gently stroked her face.
>
> "There," said his mother, "now go to bed. You'll be *so* tired in the morning." As she was speaking she heard her husband coming. "There's your father—now go." Suddenly she looked at him almost as if in fear. "Perhaps I'm selfish. If you want her, take her, my boy."

Mrs Morel is pathetic in her jealousy of Miriam, but if Miriam is not like an ordinary girl she herself hardly behaves like an ordinary mother. Under the painful stimulus of her complaints about her husband, the love between mother and son takes on a dangerously erotic character. And Mrs Morel is at least partially aware of what she is doing: with the approach of her husband she realizes, with a sudden feeling of guilt, how she has compromised her son. But her recantation is of little avail in the face of Paul's aroused passion for her. His passion seeks an outlet, and balked in the direction it would take, it turns viciously on his father. When Morel comes in, he takes a pie which Mrs Morel has specially bought for Paul, and on being challenged by her, he flings it into the fire. He too is ready for violence, for he has not mistaken the import of the scene which meets him:

> Paul started to his feet.
> "Waste your own stuff!" he cried.
> "What—what!" suddenly shouted Morel, jumping up and clenching his fist. "I'll show yer, yer young jockey!"
> "All right!" said Paul viciously, putting his head on one side. "Show me!"
> He would at that moment dearly have loved to have a smack at something. Morel was half crouching, fists up, ready to spring. The young man stood, smiling with his lips.
> "Ussha!" hissed the father, swiping round with a great stroke just past his son's face. He dared not, even though so close, really touch the young man, but swerved an inch away.
> "Right!" said Paul, his eyes upon the side of his father's mouth, where in another instant his fist would have hit. He ached for that stroke. But he heard a faint moan from behind. His mother was deadly pale, and dark at the mouth.

Paul desists, ostensibly for the sake of his mother, but within the wider context of the book as a whole it is significant that neither father nor son can actually bring himself to strike the other. Their enmity is real enough but it is the surface enmity of an unhealthy rivalry rather than that of a deep-seated personal antagonism:

"Can you go to bed, Mother?"
"Yes, I'll come."
"Sleep with Annie, Mother, not with him."
"No. I'll sleep in my own bed."
"Don't sleep with him, Mother."
"I'll sleep in my own bed."

The clash between Paul and Morel is of course a striking example of an oedipal situation, and indeed on publication the book was treated as a *locus classicus* by early English Freudians. "Yes," Frieda wrote to Frederick J. Hoffman, "Lawrence knew about Freud before he wrote the final draft of *Sons and Lovers*," but I am inclined to accept Hoffman's conclusion that "it is doubtful . . . that the revision of *Sons and Lovers* was more than superficially affected by Lawrence's introduction to psychoanalysis." At that time Lawrence's knowledge of Freudian theory was derived at second-hand from Frieda, and she probably did no more than confirm his intuitive apprehension of the nature of Paul's relations with his parents. Nor does the book betray any signs of artificial grafting.

The sort of penetrative understanding which is at work behind the organization of the scene I have just discussed informs countless incidents in the book. There is, for instance, the scene when Paul is ill as a young boy:

> On retiring to bed, the father would come into the sick-room. He was always very gentle if anyone were ill. But he disturbed the atmosphere for the boy.
> "Are ter asleep, my darlin'?" Morel asked softly.
> "No; is my mother comin'?"
> "She's just finishin' foldin' the clothes. Do you want anything?" Morel rarely "thee'd" his son.
> "I don't want nothing. But how long will she be?"
> "Not long, my duckie."
> The father waited undecidedly on the hearthrug for a moment or two. He felt his son did not want him. . . .
> He loitered about indefinitely. The boy began to get feverish with irritation. His father's presence seemed to aggravate all his sick impatience. At last Morel, after having stood looking at his son awhile, said softly:
> "Good-night, my darling."

"Good-night," Paul replied, turning round in relief to
be alone.

Paul loved to sleep with his mother. Sleep is still most
perfect, in spite of hygienists, when it is shared with a beloved. The warmth, the security and peace of soul, the
utter comfort from the touch of the other, knits the sleep,
so that it takes the body and soul completely in its healing.
Paul lay against her and slept, and got better; whilst she,
always a bad sleeper, fell later on into a profound sleep that
seemed to give her faith.

Morel, it is seen, does not have to be provocative to be rejected.
Paul's rebuffing of his father's warm gentleness and kindliness is only
understandable in terms of the inbred family situation; and indeed,
as the concluding paragraph makes clear, the conflict between father
and son which manifests itself later in an apparent readiness to come
to blows is incipient here. At this stage Paul's childish desire to sleep
with his mother is presented simply and naturally as a longing for
maternal warmth and security, but later developments are anticipated in the ambiguous phraseology of the paragraph. We are re-
minded of Lawrence's claim in the well-known letter to Edward Garnett that the development of the book "is slow, like growth." It is
only by slow stages that Paul's incestuous love for his mother expresses itself in the frankly passionate kisses of his manhood: first,
there is the seemingly childlike innocence of the foregoing scene;
then there is the more open ambiguity of his attitude as a youth. Paul
is sixteen when he falls seriously ill. It is a cruel irony that the love
which then makes him desperately assert his will to live should later
prove to be so deathly in its effects:

Paul was very ill. His mother lay in bed at nights with him;
they could not afford a nurse. He grew worse, and the
crisis approached. One night he tossed into consciousness
in the ghastly, sickly feeling of dissolution, when all the
cells in the body seem in intense irritability to be breaking
down, and consciousness makes a last flare of struggle,
like madness.

"I s'll die, mother!" he cried, heaving for breath on the
pillow.

She lifted him up, crying in a small voice:

"Oh, my son—my son!"

That brought him to. He realized her. His whole will rose up and arrested him. He put his head on her breast, and took ease of her for love.

The immediate effect of Mrs Morel's poisonously possessive love for Paul is her implacable hostility to Miriam. From the moment she senses his interest in the girl she tried to fight her off:

> Always when he went with Miriam, and it grew rather late, he knew his mother was fretting and getting angry about him—why, he could not understand. As he went into the house, flinging down his cap, his mother looked up at the clock. . . .
>
> "She must be wonderfully fascinating, that you can't get away from her, but must go trailing eight miles at this time of night."
>
> He was hurt between the past glamour with Miriam and the knowledge that his mother fretted. He had meant not to say anything, to refuse to answer. But he could not harden his heart to ignore his mother.
>
> "I *do* like to talk to her," he answered irritably.
>
> "Is there nobody else to talk to?"
>
> "You wouldn't say anything if I went with Edgar."
>
> "You know I should. You know, whoever you went with, I should say it was too far for you to go trailing, late at night, when you've been to Nottingham. Besides"— her voice suddenly flashed into anger and contempt—"it is disgusting—bits of lads and girls courting."

Paul's inability to understand Mrs Morel's antagonism to Miriam is, at this stage of the narrative, bound up with his own repressions. Struggling as he is with his complex emotions towards his mother, it is hardly surprising he should fail to realize that her jealousy is almost nakedly sexual. The real reason for her annoyance is casually phrased as an afterthought, but her sudden violent employment of the word "disgusting" and the illogical asperity of the comment itself are sure guides to her feeling. It is seldom, however, that the serpent in the garden slithers out of the undergrowth in this way; Mrs Morel effectively rationalizes her dislike of Miriam:

> "She exults—she exults as she carries him off from me," Mrs Morel cried in her heart when Paul had gone. "She's

not like an ordinary woman, who can leave me my share
in him. She wants to absorb him. She wants to draw him
out and absorb him till there is nothing left of him, even
for himself. He will never be a man on his own feet—she
will suck him up." So the mother sat, and battled and
brooded bitterly.

It is a further indication of Lawrence's comprehensive view—I
have already referred in this respect to his treatment of the Morel
marriage—that Mrs Morel's criticism of Miriam should be just; but,
as R. P. Draper has pointed out, she does not perceive its application
to herself. It is she who is preventing Paul from being a man on his
own feet, and though she is not as hostile to Clara as to Miriam, her
carping at his attachment to the married woman is parallel to
her interference in his relationship with the girl. Her approval of her
son's women is always irremediably conditional: "'You know I
should be *glad* [at your association with Clara],' she tells Paul, 'if she
weren't a married woman.'"

Since Paul cannot but agree with his mother's objections to Miriam, it is her attitude to Clara which finally makes him aware of her
possessive jealousy. Mrs Morel, asking more of Paul than he can
give, relentlessly holding him back, plays the same part as the
"beggar-woman" of "End of Another Home Holiday":

> While ever at my side,
> Frail and sad, with grey, bowed head,
> The beggar-woman, the yearning-eyed
> Inexorable love goes lagging.

Eventually Paul comes to realize that his mother is defrauding him
of life:

> Then sometimes he hated her, and pulled at her bondage.
> His life wanted to free itself of her. It was like a circle
> where life turned back on itself, and got no farther. She
> bore him, loved him, kept him, and his love turned back
> into her, so that he could not be free to go forward with
> his own life, really love another woman.

And from pulling at her bondage it is but a short step to a scarcely
disguised wish for her death:

"And as for wanting to marry," said his mother, "there's plenty of time yet."

"But no, mother. I even love Clara, and I did Miriam; but to *give* myself to them in marriage I couldn't. I couldn't belong to them. They seem to want *me,* and I can't ever give it them."

"You haven't met the right woman."

"And I never shall meet the right woman while you live," he said.

These two passages alone, quite apart from the circumstances of Mrs Morel's death which I shall discuss in a moment, should suffice to refute the criticism that in *Sons and Lovers* Lawrence capitulates to his mother. This misreading of the book derives, it would seem, from an uncritical acceptance of Jessie Chambers's verdict: "His mother conquered indeed, but the vanquished one was her son. In *Sons and Lovers* Lawrence handed his mother the laurels of victory." In her wake the froth gathers: "At the same time that the book condemns the mother it justifies her" (Mark Schorer); "the story of Paul Morel . . . was to be his mother's justification and apotheosis" (Helen Corke); "hence the distortion he made in the presentation of Miriam in his great novel, in order that the mother might triumph" (A. L. Rowse); "Lawrence was unable to detach himself from the mother whom he celebrates as heroine or to achieve the impersonality that the most personal art requires" (William York Tindall); "Lawrence tells us that Paul 'fought against his mother almost as he fought against Miriam' (chapter 9). But this statement we may disregard, for the evidence of the novel gives it the lie. He did not fight against his mother; he grew in bondage and until her death in bondage he remained" (Eliseo Vivas). It is necessary to clarify this assumption of the mother's triumph, for it underlies the even more widely accepted view that the Miriam section of the book (which remains to be discussed) is both false and a failure. Mrs Morel does have a limited triumph, in so far as Paul does not marry while she lives, but then his failure to do so is only partially attributable to her; it has as much to do with Miriam and Clara. The extent, moreover, to which Paul himself, because of his mother's influence, is to blame for the failure is fully and frankly indicated, as the two passages quoted above should make abundantly clear. And the so-called "justification" of Mrs Morel is a matter not of approbation but of truly creative presentment of character, whereby the motivating circumstances of her overpowering love for Paul are sympathetically portrayed. They may even be shown as extenuating circumstances, but that her influence is crippling—it is the theme of the book—is quite unambiguous. If it is crippling, however, it is not paralysing—as Jessie Chambers apparently believed. Paul makes his own stand for life.

There is, significantly, an image associated with the idea of crippling in the poem "Monologue of a Mother":

> Strange he is, my son, for whom I have waited like a lover;
>
> . . . .
>
> Like a thin white bird blown out of the northern seas,
> Like a bird from the far north blown with a broken wing
> Into our sooty garden, he drags and beats
> Along the fence perpetually, seeking release
> From me, from the hand of my love which creeps up,
>   needing
> His happiness, while he in displeasure retreats.

Like the son in the poem and like the bird with a broken wing, Paul also seeks release; and it is surely an Empsonian ambiguity that the chapter which describes the painful suffering and death of Mrs Morel should be entitled "The Release."

Any interpretation of *Sons and Lovers* must finally centre on this chapter, and so it is perhaps as well first to marshal the facts. Mrs Morel is stricken with cancer and her long-drawn-out suffering is so acute that Paul wishes she would die. Weeks pass and he begins to dilute her milk so that it will not nourish her. Finally, Paul decides to end her misery by giving her an overdose of morphia:

> That evening he got all the morphia pills there were, and took them downstairs. Carefully he crushed them to powder.
>
>   "What are you doing?" said Annie.
>
>   "I s'll put 'em in her night milk."
>
> Then they both laughed together like two conspiring children. On top of all their horror flickered this little sanity.

Mrs Morel lasts through the night, and Paul wonders whether her "horrible breathing" will stop if he piles "heavy clothes on top of her." She dies the next morning.

Clearly, on one level, Paul's killing of his mother is a mercy-killing. His agony at her suffering is poignantly described, and when she is dead he can only helplessly wish that she were alive again:

> She lay like a maiden asleep. . . . She would wake up. She would lift her eyelids. She was with him still. He bent and kissed her passionately. But there was coldness against his mouth. He bit his lip with horror. Looking at her, he felt he could never, never let her go. No! He stroked the hair from her temples. That, too, was cold. He saw the mouth so dumb and wondering at the hurt. Then he crouched on the floor, whispering to her:
> "Mother, mother!"

But, on a deeper level, the killing and the desire to smother his mother have a significance which he is not aware of consciously. I think we must concur with Anthony West and Graham Hough that Paul's killing of his mother represents, symbolically, both a repudiation of what she stands for and a decisive act of self-liberation, as does his turning towards the city at the end of the book:

> But no, he would not give in. Turning sharply, he walked towards the city's gold phosphorescence. His fists were shut, his mouth set fast. He would not take that direction, to the darkness, to follow her. He walked towards the faintly humming, glowing town, quickly.

I believe that a close textual analysis of the passage, quoted above, which describes the preparation of the death-draught, reveals further significances of the killing. It will be recalled that, when Paul tells Annie that he intends to give Mrs Morel the morphia, "they both laughed together," and that their laughter is described as the flickering of a "little sanity": it suggests, then, not only the tension they feel and their instinctive ("sane") need for some relief from their oppressive horror, but also the sanity-in defiance of established law—which the mercy-killing represents. They are also said, however, to laugh "like two conspiring children." Taken together with the fact that Paul replies to Annie's question in the dialect of his youth, the simile, I think, points back to an earlier and apparently irrelevant incident which illuminates the meaning of Paul's killing of his mother.

The only childhood "conspiracy" in which Paul and Annie can be said to engage occurs when he decides to burn her doll, which he has accidentally smashed. The "flickering" of Paul's "sanity," it seems, should ultimately be related to the flames in which the doll is "sacrificed":

> "You couldn't tell it was there, mother; you couldn't tell it was there," he repeated over and over. So long as Annie wept for the doll he sat helpless with misery. Her grief wore itself out. She forgave her brother—he was so much upset. But a day or two afterwards she was shocked.
>
> "Let's make a sacrifice of Arabella," he said. "Let's burn her."
>
> She was horrified, yet rather fascinated. She wanted to see what the boy would do. He made an altar of bricks, pulled some of the shavings out of Arabella's body, put the waxen fragments into the hollow face, poured on a little paraffin, and set the whole thing alight. He watched with wicked satisfaction the drops of wax melt off the broken forehead of Arabella, and drop like sweat into the flame. So long as the stupid big doll burned he rejoiced in silence. At the end he poked among the embers with a stick, fished out the arms and legs, all blackened, and smashed them under stones.
>
> "That's the sacrifice of Missis Arabella," he said. "An' I'm glad there's nothing left of her."
>
> Which disturbed Annie inwardly, although she could say nothing. He seemed to hate the doll so intensely, because he had broken it.

Child psychologists, I imagine, would find the symbolism of this burning of the doll familiar. The "wicked satisfaction" which Paul derives from his violent and compulsive destruction of the doll is surely not unrelated to the fact that he calls the "big" doll "Missis" Arabella and that the melted wax of its forehead drops "like sweat" into the flame. But I am not so much concerned with the burning of the doll as an expression of a childhood wish to destroy the mother as with its relation to the actual killing which takes place later. First, we might note, in passing, the analogy between Paul's smashing of the arms and legs of the doll after the burning and his urge to smother his mother after she has already taken the morphia. Second, he hates and destroys the doll "because he [has] broken it"; in other words, the "sacrifice" represents some sort of expiation—as, in a measure, the killing is an unconscious purgation of the feelings of guilt which his ambiguous relationship with his mother has necessarily involved. Third, the burning of the doll seems to represent a childish but resolute refusal to sacrifice himself to it. In the same way, the killing, in one of its complex meanings, is a decisive protest against the self-sacrifice which subjection to his mother has entailed:

> And he came back to her. And in his soul was a feeling of
> the satisfaction of self-sacrifice because he was faithful to
> her. She loved him first; he loved her first. And yet it was
> not enough. His new young life, so strong and imperious,
> was urged towards something else. It made him mad with
> restlessness.

Indeed, the pernicious effect of self-sacrifice is an insistent theme in the novel. Mrs Morel's married life is almost wholly self-sacrificial, involving as it does unwilling service of her husband, and despite her possessive love for Paul, abnegation of self for the sake of her children. In fact her self-sacrifice borders, masochistically, on the self-destructive:

> "Are you sure it's a tumour?" [Paul asked Dr Ansell].
> "Why did Dr Jameson in Nottingham never find out any-
> thing about it? She's been going to him for weeks, and he's
> treated her for heart and indigestion."
> "Mrs Morel never told Dr Jameson about the lump,"
> said the doctor.

Mrs Morel is the embodiment of a principle which Lawrence fought against all his life, and in refusing to sacrifice himself to her, Paul repudiates a great deal of what she stands for. Nor is Paul's fight against self-sacrifice confined to his relations with his mother; it is also at the heart of his conflict with Miriam. It is perhaps significant that, of all the major characters, Walter Morel is the only one who doggedly pursues his own way, neither sacrificing himself for others nor expecting that they should sacrifice themselves for him.

Sons and Lovers, then, forcefully suggests Paul's ultimate rejection of his mother; it also implies his unconscious identification with his father. As far as his father is concerned, there are no dramatic manifestations of feeling comparable to his killing of his mother and his turning towards the town at the end of the book, but his identification with him is none the less unmistakable. It shows itself, for instance, in his unconscious imitation of his father's mannerisms—when Morel greets Clara she sees "Paul's manner of bowing and shaking hands"—and, more explicitly, in his reflections on class:

"You know," he said to his mother, "I don't want to belong to the well-to-do middle class. I like my common people best. I belong to the common people."

"But if anyone else said so, my son, wouldn't you be in a tear. *You* know you consider yourself equal to any gentleman."

"In myself," he answered, "not in my class or my education or my manners. But in myself I am."

"Very well, then. Then why talk about the common people?"

"Because—the difference between people isn't in their class, but in themselves. Only from the middle classes one gets ideas, and from the common people—life itself, warmth. You feel their hates and loves."

"It's all very well, my boy. But, then, why don't you go and talk to your father's pals?"

"But they're rather different."

"Not at all. They're the common people. After all, whom do you mix with now—among the common people? Those that exchange ideas, like the middle classes. The rest don't interest you."

"But—there's the life—"

"I don't believe there's a jot more life from Miriam than you could get from any educated girl—say Miss Moreton. It is *you* who are snobbish about class."

Paul's ideas about class, it may be remarked, are a rough statement of the sort of clash which is dramatized in *Lady Chatterley's Lover;* they also point to the way in which he is drawn to his father. There is of course a lot in what Mrs Morel says, and Paul finds it difficult to define his feelings and to explain his reluctance to associate with his "father's pals," but if he could bring himself to own it, it is clearly his father—and not Miriam, as Mrs Morel jealously and falsely supposes—who is the prototype of his image of the "common people" (to whom he feels he belongs) and who embodies the vitality and exuberance and warmth which evoke his deepest sympathies. And despite his antipathy towards his father, he recognizes what it is that Morel has given his wife: the "real, real flame of feeling" which he tells Miriam his mother has experienced "through" his father is simply an alternative phrase for "life itself, warmth," for that quality which he tries to convince his mother the working class possesses.

I think it is fair to assume that the depiction of Paul's relations with his mother and father is a reliable guide to the nature of Lawrence's feelings about his own parents. Certainly there is wide agreement about his unconscious identification with his father in real life and in the work which follows *Sons and Lovers.* And Lawrence himself, though he phrases the affirmation obliquely, attests the vital nature of the bond which existed between him and his father:

> If the large parent mother-germ still lives and acts vividly and mysteriously in the great fused nucleus of your solar plexus, does the smaller, brilliant male-spark that derived from your father act any less vividly? By no means. It is different—it is less ostensible. It may be even in magnitude smaller. But it may be even more vivid, even more intrinsic. So beware how you deny the father-quick of yourself. You may be denying the most intrinsic quick of all.
>
> (*Fantasia of the Unconscious*)

It is also instructive, I think, to compare the following two passages, the first from *Sons and Lovers,* the second from a letter written a few months after the completion of the novel:

> Gertrude Coppard had watched [Morel], fascinated. He was so full of colour and animation, his voice ran so easily into comic grotesque, he was so ready and so pleasant with everybody. Her own father had a rich fund of humour, but it was satiric. This man's was different: soft, non-intellectual, warm, a kind of gambolling.
>
> She herself was opposite. She had a curious, receptive mind, which found much pleasure and amusement in listening to other folk. She was clever in leading folk on to talk. She loved ideas, and was considered very intellectual. What she liked most of all was an argument on religion or philosophy or politics with some educated man. . . .
>
> She was a puritan, like her father, high-minded, and really stern. Therefore the dusky, golden softness of this

man's sensuous flame of life, that flowed off his flesh like the flame from a candle, not baffled and gripped into incandescence by thought and spirit as her life was, seemed to her something wonderful, beyond her.

I conceive a man's body as a kind of flame, like a candle flame, forever upright and yet flowing: and the intellect is just the light that is shed on to the things around. And I am not so much concerned with the things around—which is really mind—but with the mystery of the flame forever flowing, coming God knows how from out of practically nowhere, and being *itself,* whatever there is around it, that it lights up.

The recurrence of the striking candle flame image, with its suggestion of glowing warmth and mysterious being, signifies yet again a link between what Lawrence's father was (I think it is safe, at this stage, to identify the characters with their prototypes in real life) and what he himself was most concerned with. And it was not to his mother alone, we sense, that what the miner was "seemed something wonderful." But there are other implications to the passage quoted from the novel. What it vividly suggests is the strength of the impulse by which the young couple are attracted to their opposites, and the opposition described is so radical that it clearly must have had an important influence on Lawrence himself. Indeed Diana Trilling declares that, "identifying himself now with the one parent, now with the other, Lawrence tried throughout his life to understand and to reconstitute in his own person their unhappy marriage"; and Richard Rees follows her in believing that Lawrence's "attempt to balance the scale [of values represented by his parents] was to be an important part of his life's work." The views of these critics link up, at one point, with those advanced [elsewhere in] this discussion, but the difference between us is precisely that which I wish to pursue in the analysis of Lawrence's development subsequent to the writing of *Sons and Lovers*. This seminal novel suggests the personal significance of Lawrence's formulation some two years later (in the Hardy essay) of the male and female principles. . . . Lawrence's formulation of the female principle as a complement of the male principle may therefore be viewed as an attempt to give full weight to qualities which his father embodied and which were underrated in his own home. Indeed the value accorded the female principle is a measure of his liberation from his mother's dominance. But the fact that his father is associated with the female principle and his mother with the male is also suggestive of the cause of the breach in his own nature. It is this breach which made it imperative for him to try to reconcile the opposing qualities within himself. The novels after *Sons and Lovers* are a record of this struggle and of the violent negations it engendered.

Portrait of Miriam

Louis L. Martz

The girl was romantic in her soul.

And she was cut off from ordinary life by her religious intensity which made the world for her either a nunnery garden or a paradise, where sin and knowledge were not, or else an ugly, cruel thing.

And in sacrifice she was proud, in renunciation she was strong, for she did not trust herself to support everyday life.

"You don't want to love—your eternal and abnormal craving is to be loved. You aren't positive, you're negative. You absorb, absorb, as if you must fill yourself up with love, because you've got a shortage somewhere."

With very few exceptions, the commentators on Lawrence's *Sons and Lovers* have tended to accept the view of Miriam's character as thus described by the narrator and by Paul Morel. Mark Spilka, for example, in his stimulating book, bases his interpretation of the novel on the assumption that Miriam has "an unhealthy spirituality," is truly "negative," that she really "wheedles the soul out of things," as Paul Morel says, and that "because of the stifling nature of Miriam's love, Paul refuses to marry her"—justifiably, since "Miriam's fri-

---

From *Imagined Worlds: Essays on Some English Novels and Novelists in Honour of John Butt*, edited by Maynard Mack and Ian Gregor. © 1968 by Methuen & Co., Ltd.

gidity is rooted in her own nature." But I believe that the portrait of Miriam is far more complex than either Paul or the narrator will allow, and that a study of her part in the book will cast some light upon the puzzling and peculiar technique of narration that Lawrence adopts when he comes to the central section of his novel, the five tormented chapters (7–11) running from "Lad-and-Girl Love" through "The Test on Miriam."

As everyone has noticed, part 1 of the novel (the first third of the book, concluding with the death of William) is written in the manner of Victorian realism: the omniscient narrator, working with firm control, sets forth the facts objectively. The countryside, the mining village, the family conflicts, the daily life of the household—all is given in clear, precise, convincing detail. The use of local dialect, the echoes of biblical style, the short, concise sentences combine to create in us a confidence in the narrator's command of his materials. His fairness to everyone is evident. If the father is predominantly shown as brutal and drunken, in those savage quarrels with the mother, he is also shown in his younger glory as a man who might have flourished with a different wife: "Gertrude Coppard watched the young miner as he danced, a certain subtle exultation like glamour in his movement, and his face the flower of his body, ruddy, with tumbled black hair, and laughing alike whatever partner he bowed above." Even when the wife has turned away from him she can enjoy his music:

> Quite early, before six o'clock, she heard him whistling away to himself downstairs. He had a pleasant way of whistling, lively and musical. He nearly always whistled hymns. He had been a choir-boy with a beautiful voice, and had taken solos in Southwell cathedral. His morning whistling alone betrayed it.
>
> His wife lay listening to him tinkering away in the garden, his whistling ringing out as he sawed and hammered away. It always gave her a sense of warmth and peace to hear him thus as she lay in bed, the children not yet awake, in the bright early morning, happy in his man's fashion.

We watch Morel's relish in getting his breakfast and his joy in walking across the fields to his work in the early morning; we learn of those happy times when Morel is cobbling the family's boots, or mending kettles, or making fuses; we recognize his faithful labour at his gruelling job; and particularly we notice the love for him felt by the youngest child Arthur: "Mrs. Morel was glad this child loved the father." All these things give a sense of balance and proportion to part 1, making it clear that Paul's view is partial, unfair to the father, ignoring his basic humanity.

Paul's blindness towards his father's very existence as a human being is cruelly shown in the scene where Morel emerges from the pit to hear of William's death:

> "And William is dead, and my mother's in London, and what will she be doing?" the boy asked himself, as if it were a conundrum.
>
> He watched chair after chair come up, and still no father. At last, standing beside a waggon, a man's form! The chair sank on its rests, Morel stepped off. He was slightly lame from an accident.
>
> "Is it thee, Paul? Is 'e worse?"
>
> "You've got to go to London."
>
> The two walked off the pit-bank, where men were watching curiously. As they came out and went along the railway, with the sunny autumn field on one side and a wall of trucks on the other, Morel said in a frightened voice:
>
> "'E's niver gone, child?"
>
> "Yes."
>
> "When wor't?"
>
> The miner's voice was terrified.
>
> "Last night. We had a telegram from my mother."
>
> Morel walked on a few strides, then leaned up against a truck side, his hand over his eyes. He was not crying. Paul stood looking round, waiting. On the weighing-machine a truck trundled slowly. Paul saw everything, except his father leaning against the truck as if he were tired.

"Paul saw everything, except his father." Only the omniscient narrator reveals the man Morel, battered from his work, frightened for his son's life, sunk in dumb agony at the news, while his intimate dialect plays off pitifully against the formal language of Paul, to stress the total division between the two.

Part 1, then, is a triumph of narration in the old Victorian style. It is a long prologue, in which the issues are clearly defined, and in which, above all, the mother's overpowering influence is shown in the death of one son, while she turns toward Paul as her only remaining hope: "'I should have watched the living, not the dead,' she told herself."

Meanwhile, as William is engaged in his fatal courtship, the figure of Miriam has been quietly introduced, in the natural, harmonious setting of the farm: "Mother and son went into the small railed garden, where was a scent of red gillivers. By the open door were some floury loaves, put out to cool. A hen was just coming to peck them. Then, in the doorway suddenly appeared a girl in a dirty apron. She was about fourteen years old, had a rosy dark face, a bunch of short black curls, very fine and free, and dark eyes; shy, questioning, a little resentful of the strangers, she disappeared." Shortly after this follows the vivid incident in which the brothers jeer at Miriam for being afraid to let the hen peck the corn out of her hand:

> "Now, Miriam," said Maurice, "you come an' 'ave a go."
>
> "No," she cried, shrinking back.
>
> "Ha! baby. The mardy-kid!" said her brothers.
>
> "It doesn't hurt a bit," said Paul. "It only just nips rather nicely."
>
> "No," she still cried, shaking her black curls and shrinking.
>
> "She dursn't," said Geoffrey. "She niver durst do anything except recite poitry."
>
> "Dursn't jump off a gate, dursn't tweedle, dursn't go on a slide, dursn't stop a girl hittin' her. She can do nowt but go about thinkin' herself somebody. 'The Lady of the Lake.' Yah!" cried Maurice.

We are bound to align this with the later incident of the swing, both of which might be taken "as revelations of Miriam's diminished vitality, her tendency to shrink back from life, whether she is making love, feeding chickens, trying to cope with Mrs. Morel's dislike of her, or merely looking at flowers." But we should note that immediately after the passage just quoted Paul witnesses another aspect of Miriam:

> As he went round the back, he saw Miriam kneeling in front of the hen-coop, some maize in her hand, biting her

lip, and crouching in an intense attitude. The hen was eye-
ing her wickedly. Very gingerly she put forward her hand.
The hen bobbed for her. She drew back quickly with a cry,
half of fear, half of chagrin.

"It won't hurt you," said Paul.

She flushed crimson and started up.

"I only wanted to try," she said in a low voice.

"See, it doesn't hurt," he said, and, putting only two
corns in his palm, he let the hen peck, peck, peck at his
bare hand. "It only makes you laugh," he said.

She put her hand forward, and dragged it away, tried
again, and started back with a cry. He frowned.

"Why, I'd let her take corn from my face," said Paul,
"only she bumps a bit. She's ever so neat. If she wasn't,
look how much ground she'd peck up every day."

He waited grimly, and watched. At last Miriam let the
bird peck from her hand. She gave a little cry—fear, and
pain because of fear—rather pathetic. But she had done it,
and she did it again.

"There, you see," said the boy. "It doesn't hurt, does it?"

She looked at him with dilated dark eyes.

"No," she laughed, trembling.

The scene shows more than timidity; it shows, also, her extreme
sensitivity, along with her shy desire for new experience: she wants
to try, she wants to learn; if rightly encouraged she will and can
learn, and then she can respond with laughter and trembling excitement. This first view of Miriam, seen through the eyes of the objective narrator, is astir with life: for all her shyness and shrinking she
is nevertheless capable of a strong response. The whole initial sketch
is suffused with her "beautiful warm colouring" and accompanied
by her "musical, quiet voice." She is a girl of rich potential.

II

As part 2 opens we become at once aware of a drastic shift in
method. The first two pages are given over to an elaborate interpretation of Miriam's character before she again appears, "nearly sixteen, very beautiful, with her warm colouring, her gravity, her eyes

dilating suddenly like an ecstasy." No such extended analysis of anyone has appeared in part 1; there the characters have been allowed to
act out their parts before us, with only brief guiding touches by the
objective narrator. But here we sense a peculiar intensity in the analysis: the narrator seems to be preparing the way for some new and
difficult problem, and in so doing he seems to be dropping his manner of impartiality. He is determined to set our minds in a certain
direction, and this aim is reflected in the drifting length and involu-
tion of the sentences. The style of writing here seems designed to
reflect the "mistiness" of the character he is describing, her remote-
ness from life:

> Her great companion was her mother. They were both
> brown-eyed, and inclined to be mystical, such women as
> treasure religion inside them, breathe it in their nostrils,
> and see the whole of life in a mist thereof. So to Miriam,
> Christ and God made one great figure, which she loved
> tremblingly and passionately when a tremendous sunset
> burned out the western sky, and Ediths, and Lucys, and
> Rowenas, Brian de Bois Guilberts, Rob Roys, and Guy
> Mannerings, rustled the sunny leaves in the morning, or
> sat in her bedroom aloft, alone, when it snowed. That was
> life to her. For the rest, she drudged in the house, which
> work she would not have minded had not her clean red
> floor been mucked up immediately by the trampling farm-
> boots of her brothers. She madly wanted her little brother
> of four to let her swathe him and stifle him in her love; she
> went to church reverently, with bowed head, and quivered
> in anguish from the vulgarity of the other choir-girls and
> from the common-sounding voice of the curate; she
> fought with her brothers, whom she considered brutal
> louts; and she held not her father in too high esteem be-
> cause he did not carry any mystical ideals cherished in his
> heart, but only wanted to have as easy a time as he could,
> and his meals when he was ready for them.

She is also a girl who is "mad to have learning whereon to pride
herself"; and for all these causes she neglects and ignores her physical
being: "Her beauty—that of a shy, wild, quiveringly sensitive
thing—seemed nothing to her. Even her soul, so strong for rhap-
sody, was not enough. She must have something to reinforce her

pride, because she felt different from other people." At the same time, her misty emotions lead her towards a desire to dominate Paul: "Then he was so ill, and she felt he would be weak. Then she would be stronger than he. Then she could love him. If she could be mistress of him in his weakness, take care of him, if he could depend on her, if she could, as it were, have him in her arms, how she would love him!"

In all this the narrator is anticipating the views of Miriam frequently expressed by Paul himself: that she is too spiritual, too abstract, that she shrinks away from physical reality, and that she has a stifling desire to absorb and possess his soul. The incident of the swing that follows shortly after would seem to bear out some of this: she is afraid to let Paul swing her high, and Lawrence phrases her fear in language that has unmistakable sexual overtones: "She felt the accuracy with which he caught her, exactly at the right moment, and the exactly proportionate strength of his thrust, and she was afraid. Down to her bowels went the hot wave of fear. She was in his hands. Again, firm and inevitable came the thrust at the right moment. She gripped the rope, almost swooning." Yet she has led Paul to the swing, and she is fascinated by his free swinging: "It roused a warmth in her. It were almost as if he were a flame that had lit a warmth in her whilst he swung in the middle air." Who can say that Miriam is unable to learn this too, as she has learned with the hen, and as she is later shown to overcome her fear of crossing fences?

> Occasionally she ran with Paul down the fields. Then her eyes blazed naked in a kind of esctasy that frightened him. But she was physically afraid. If she were getting over a stile, she gripped his hands in a little hard anguish, and began to lose her presence of mind. And he could not persuade her to jump from even a small height. Her eyes dilated, became exposed and palpitating.
>
> "No!" she cried, half laughing in terror—"no!"
>
> "You shall!" he cried once, and, jerking her forward, he brought her falling from the fence. But her wild "Ah!" of pain, as if she were losing consciousness, cut him. She landed on her feet safely, and afterwards had courage in this respect.

Certainly she wants to learn; only a few lines after the swing episode we find this all-important passage:

But the girl gradually sought him out. If he brought up his sketchbook, it was she who pondered longest over the last picture. Then she would look up at him. Suddenly, her dark eyes alight like water that shakes with a stream of gold in the dark, she would ask:

"Why do I like this so?"

Always something in his breast shrank from these close, intimate, dazzled looks of hers.

"Why *do* you?" he asked.

"I don't know. It seems so true."

"It's because—it's because there is scarcely any shadow in it; it's more shimmery, as if I'd painted the shimmering protoplasm in the leaves and everywhere, and not the stiffness of the shape. That seems dead to me. Only this shimmeriness is the real living. The shape is a dead crust. The shimmer is inside really."

And she, with her little finger in her mouth, would ponder these sayings. They gave her a feeling of life again, and vivified things which had meant nothing to her. She managed to find some meaning in his struggling, abstract speeches. And they were the medium through which she came distinctly at her beloved objects.

It seems as though she is learning to reach out towards the "shimmeriness" that is the "real living"; with his help she is coming out of her "mist" towards a distinct sight of "her beloved objects." *She* is learning, while *he* shrinks away from her intimate, shimmering eyes ("like water that shakes with a stream of gold in the dark"). She senses the meaning of his "abstract speeches," she gets "so near him," she creates in him "a strange, roused sensation"—and as a result she enrages him for reasons that he cannot grasp. Is it because he is refusing to face the shimmer that is really inside Miriam?

So, when he sees her embracing her youngest brother "almost as if she were in a trance, and swaying also as if she were swooned in an ecstasy of love," he bursts out with his irritation:

"What do you make such a *fuss* for?" cried Paul, all in suffering because of her extreme emotion. "Why can't you be ordinary with him?"

She let the child go, and rose, and said nothing. Her intensity, which would leave no emotion on a normal plane, irritated the youth into a frenzy. And this fearful, naked contact of her on small occasions shocked him. He was used to his mother's reserve. And on such occasions he was thankful in his heart and soul that he had his mother, so sane and wholesome.

One senses, as Miriam does at a later point, an alien influence here, twisting the mind of Paul and the narrator away from Miriam. Two pages later we see a dramatic juxtaposition of two warring actualities:

> He used to tell his mother all these things.
> "I'm going to teach Miriam algebra," he said.
> "Well," replied Mrs. Morel, "I hope she'll get fat on it."
> When he went up to the farm on the Monday evening, it was drawing twilight. Miriam was just sweeping up the kitchen, and was kneeling at the hearth when he entered. Everyone was out but her. She looked round at him, flushed, her dark eyes shining, her fine hair falling about her face.
> "Hello!" she said, soft and musical. "I knew it was you."
> "How?"
> "I knew your step. Nobody treads so quick and firm."
> He sat down, sighing.
> "Ready to do some algebra?" he asked, drawing a little book from his pocket.

Who is sane and wholesome, we may well ask? And whose thoughts are abstracted from life? We are beginning to learn that we cannot wholly trust the narrator's remarks in this central portion of the book, for his commentary represents mainly an extension of Paul's consciousness; everywhere, in this portion of the book, the voice of the narrator tends to echo and magnify the confusions that are arising within Paul himself. These are the contradictions in which some readers have seen a failure or a faltering in the novel, because "the point of view is never adequately objectified and sustained to tell us which is true." But I feel rather that Lawrence has invented a successful technique by which he can manage the deep autobiographical problems that underlie the book. We are watching the strong graft of a stream of consciousness growing out of the live trunk of that Victorian prologue, and intertwining with the objectively presented action. The point of view adopted is that of Paul; but since confu-

sion, self-deception, and desperate self-justification are essential to
that point of view, we can never tell, from that stream of consciousness alone, where the real truth lies. But we can tell it from the action; we can tell it by seeking out the portrait of Miriam that lies
beneath the over-painted commentary of the Paul-narrator. This
technique of painting and overpainting produces a strange and
unique tension in this part of the novel. The image of Miriam appears and then is clouded over; it is as though we were looking at her
through a clouded window that is constantly being cleared, and
fogged, and cleared again. It is an unprecedented and inimitable
technique, discovered for this one necessary occasion. But it works.

How it works, we may see by looking once again at the frequently quoted passage where Miriam leads Paul, despite his reluctance ("They grumble so if I'm late") into the woods at dusk to find
the "wild-rose bush she had discovered."

> The tree was tall and straggling. It had thrown its briers
> over a hawthorn-bush, and its long streamers trailed thick,
> right down to the grass, splashing the darkness every-
> where with great split stars, pure white. In bosses of ivory
> and in large splashed stars the roses gleamed on the dark-
> ness of foliage and stems and grass. Paul and Miriam stood
> close together, silent, and watched. Point after point the
> steady roses shone out to them, seeming to kindle some-
> thing in their souls. The dusk came like smoke around,
> and still did not put out the roses.
>
> Paul looked into Miriam's eyes. She was pale and ex-
> pectant with wonder, her lips were parted, and her dark
> eyes lay open to him. His look seemed to travel down into
> her. Her soul quivered. It was the communion she wanted.
> He turned aside, as if pained. He turned to the bush.
>
> "They seem as if they walk like butterflies, and shake
> themselves," he said.
>
> She looked at her roses. They were white, some in-
> curved and holy, others expanded in an ecstasy. The tree
> was dark as a shadow. She lifted her hand impulsively to
> the flowers; she went forward and touched them in
> worship.
>
> "Let us go," he said.
>
> There was a cool scent of ivory roses—a white, virgin

scent. Something made him feel anxious and imprisoned. The two walked in silence.

What is this "something" that makes him "feel anxious and imprisoned"? Is he like the hawthorn-bush, caught in the trailing streamers of the rose-bush? Is it because she has insisted on a moment of soul-communion which represents her tendency towards "a blasphemous possessorship"? The narrator seems to be urging us in this direction. Yet in itself the scene may be taken to represent, amid this wild profusion of natural growth, a moment of natural communion in the human relationship, a potential marriage of senses and the soul. This is, for Miriam, an "ecstasy" in which nature is not abstracted, but realized in all its wild perfection. Paul breaks the mood and runs away towards home. And when he reaches home we may grasp the true manner of his imprisonment:

> Always when he went with Miriam, and it grew rather late, he knew his mother was fretting and getting angry about him—why, he could not understand. As he went into the house, flinging down his cap, his mother looked up at the clock. She had been sitting thinking because a chill to her eyes prevented her reading. She could feel Paul being drawn away by this girl. And she did not care for Miriam. "She is one of those who will want to suck a man's soul out till he has none of his own left," she said to herself; "and he is just such a gaby as to let himself be absorbed. She will never let him become a man; she never will." So, while he was away with Miriam, Mrs. Morel grew more and more worked up.
>
> She glanced at the clock and said, coldly and rather tired:
>
> "You have been far enough to-night."
>
> His soul, warm and exposed from contact with the girl, shrank.

Miriam offers him the freedom of natural growth within a mature relation, though Paul soon adopts the mother's view of Miriam's "possessive" nature. He cannot help himself, but there is no reason why readers of the book should accept the mother's view of Miriam, which is everywhere shown to be motivated by the mother's own possessiveness. The mother has described only herself in the above quotation; she has not described Miriam, who is quite a different being and has quite a different effect on Paul. The fact is that Paul needs both his mother and Miriam for his true development, as he seems to realize quite early in the conflict: "A sketch finished, he always wanted to take it to Miriam. Then he was stimulated into knowledge of the work he had produced unconsciously. In contact with Miriam he gained insight; his vision went deeper. From his mother he drew the life-warmth, the strength to produce; Miriam urged this warmth into intensity like a white light." Or earlier we hear that Miriam's family "kindled him and made him glow to his work, whereas his mother's influence was to make him quietly determined, patient, dogged, unwearied."

But the mother cannot bear to release him. Miriam must be met by her with cold, unfriendly curtness, while the married woman, Clara, may receive a friendly welcome from the mother. Clara offers no threat: "Mrs. Morel measured herself against the younger woman, and found herself easily stronger." "Yes, I liked her", she says in answer to Paul's inquiry. "But you'll tire of her, my son; you know you will." And so she encourages the affair with Clara: the adulterous relation will serve the son's physical needs, while the mother can retain the son's deeper love and loyalty. Mrs. Morel senses what she is doing, but evades the facts:

> Mrs. Morel considered. She would have been glad now for her son to fall in love with some woman who would—she did not know what. But he fretted so, got so furious suddenly, and again was melancholic. She wished he knew some nice woman—She did not know what she wished, but left it vague. At any rate she was not hostile to the idea of Clara.

The mother's devices are pitiful, and at the same time contemptible, as we have already seen from the painful episode in which she overwhelms her son with raw and naked emotion:

> He had taken off his collar and tie, and rose, bare-throated, to go to bed. As he stooped to kiss his mother, she threw her arms around his neck, hid her face on his shoulder, and cried, in a whimpering voice, so unlike her own that he writhed in agony:
> "I can't bear it. I could let another woman—but not her. She'd leave me no room, not a bit of room—"
> And immediately he hated Miriam bitterly.

"And I've never—you know, Paul—I've never had a husband—not really—"

He stroked his mother's hair, and his mouth was on her throat.

"And she exults so in taking you from me—she's not like ordinary girls."

"Well, I don't love her, mother," he murmured, bowing his head and hiding his eyes on her shoulder in misery. His mother kissed him a long, fervent kiss.

"My boy!" she said, in a voice trembling with passionate love.

"At your mischief again?" says the father, "venomously," as he interrupts this scene of illicitly possessive passion. Mischief it is, corrosive and destructive to the marriage that Paul needs, the full relationship that Miriam offers, with her intimate love for nature.

It will be evident that I do not agree with the view that Spilka and others have taken of that flower-picking episode with Miriam and Clara, the view that takes the scene as a revelation of a basic flaw in Miriam: "She kills life and has no right to it."

"Ah!" cried Miriam, and she looked at Paul, her dark eyes dilating. He smiled. Together they enjoyed the field of flowers. Clara, a little way off, was looking at the cowslips disconsolately. Paul and Miriam stayed close together, talking in subdued tones. He kneeled on one knee, quickly gathering the best blossoms, moving from tuft to tuft restlessly, talking softly all the time. Miriam plucked the flowers lovingly, lingering over them. He always seemed to her too quick and almost scientific. Yet his bunches had a natural beauty more than hers. He loved them, but as if they were his and he had a right to them. She had more reverence for them: they held something she had not.

The last clause has a wonderful ambiguity. If we take Paul's point of view, we will say that she is "negative," that she lacks true life. If we ponder the whole action of the book, we will say that what she lacks is the full organic life of the flower, sexually complete within itself. She cannot grow into her full life without the principle that Paul, with his masculine creativity, here displays. The passage shows a man and a woman who are true counterparts, in mind and body. When, a little later, Paul sprinkles the flowers over Clara, he is performing an exclusively sensuous ritual that threatens more than a pagan love-death:

> Her breasts swung slightly in her blouse. The arching curve of her back was beautiful and strong; she wore no stays. Suddenly, without knowing, he was scattering a handful of cowslips over her hair and neck, saying:
>
> > "Ashes to ashes, and dust to dust,
> > If the Lord won't have you the devil must."
>
> The chill flowers fell on her neck. She looked up at him, with almost pitiful, scared grey eyes, wondering what he was doing. Flowers fell on her face, and she shut her eyes.
> Suddenly, standing there above her, he felt awkward.
> "I thought you wanted a funeral," he said, ill at ease.

It is Paul, under his mother's domination, who kills life, by refusing to move in organic relation with Miriam:

> He would not have it that they were lovers. The intimacy between them had been kept so abstract, such a matter of the soul, all thought and weary struggle into consciousness, that he saw it only as a platonic friendship. He stoutly denied there was anything else between them. Miriam was silent, or else she very quietly agreed. He was a fool who did not know what was happening to himself. By tacit agreement they ignored the remarks and insinuations of their acquaintances.
> "We aren't lovers, we are friends," he said to her. "*We* know it. Let them talk. What does it matter what they say."
> Sometimes, as they were walking together, she slipped her arm timidly into his. But he always resented it, and she knew it. It caused a violent conflict in him. With Miriam he was always on the high plane of abstraction, when his natural fire of love was transmitted into the fine steam of thought. She would have it so.

The last sentence is a fine example of the way in which the commentary of the Paul-narrator can contradict the tenor of the action: "She slipped her arm timidly into his." Clara knows better and tells Paul the truth in that revealing conversation just before "the test on Miriam." Paul has been describing how Miriam "wants the soul out of my body": "I know she wants a sort of soul union."

> "But how do you know what she wants?"
> "I've been with her for seven years."
> "And you haven't found out the very first thing about her."
> "What's that?"
> "That she doesn't want any of your soul communion. That's your own imagination. She wants you."
> He pondered over this. Perhaps he was wrong.
> "But she seems—" he began.
> "You've never tried," she answered.

This is not to deny that Miriam is shy, intense, spiritual, and, as a result of her upbringing, fearful and evasive of sexual facts. All these qualities belong to her character, for she is young, sensitive, and modest. My point is that her portrait does not consist simply of a static presentation of these aspects: her portrait is being enriched dynamically and progressively before our eyes, over a long period of years, from her early adolescence, through an awakening and potential fulfilment, to the utter extinction of her inner life and hope.

The truth of Clara's view has been borne out long before, as far back as that scene where Paul accuses Miriam of never laughing real laughter:

> "But"—and she looked up at him with eyes frightened and struggling—"I do laugh at you—I *do*."
> "Never! There's always a kind of intensity. When you laugh I could always cry; it seems as if it shows up your suffering. Oh, you make me knit the brows of my very soul and cogitate."
> Slowly she shook her head despairingly.
> "I'm sure I don't want to," she said.
> "I'm so damned spiritual with *you* always!" he cried.
> She remained silent, thinking, "Then why don't you be otherwise." But he saw her crouching, brooding figure, and it seemed to tear him in two.

And then, on the next page, as Paul repairs the bicycle tyre, we have an unmistakable glimpse of the vital image of Miriam, her strong physical feeling for him, and her true laughter:

> "Fetch me a drop of water in a bowl," he said to her. "I shall be late, and then I s'll catch it."
>
> He lighted the hurricane lamp, took off his coat, turned up the bicycle, and set speedily to work. Miriam came with the bowl of water and stood close to him, watching. She loved to see his hands doing things. He was slim and vigorous, with a kind of easiness even in his most hasty movements. And busy at his work, he seemed to forget her. She loved him absorbedly. She wanted to run her hands down his sides. She always wanted to embrace him, so long as he did not want her.
>
> "There!" he said, rising suddenly. "Now, could you have done it quicker?"
>
> "No!" she laughed.
>
> He straightened himself. His back was towards her. She put her two hands on his sides, and ran them quickly down.
>
> "You are so *fine!*" she said.
>
> He laughed, hating her voice, but his blood roused to a wave of flame by her hands. She did not seem to realise *him* in all this. He might have been an object. She never realised the male he was.

Those last three sentences, the outgrowth of his torment, and the earlier remark, "so long as he did not want her," provide clear examples of the way in which the overpainted commentary tends to obscure the basic portrait of Miriam. It is the same in the episode at Nethermere: "He could not bear to look at Miriam. She seemed to want him, and he resisted. He resisted all the time. He wanted now to give her passion and tenderness, and he could not. He felt that she wanted the soul out of his body, and not him."

> He went on, in his dead fashion:
>
> "If only you could want *me,* and not want what I can reel off for you!"
>
> "I!" she cried bitterly—"I! Why, when would you let me take you?"

His bursts of anger and "hate," his feeling that Miriam is pulling the soul out of his body, are only his own tormented reactions to the agony he feels in being pulled so strongly away from his mother, as Daniel Weiss has said: "It is that for the first time in his life he is facing a mature relationship between himself and another woman, *not* his mother, and that a different mode of love is being demanded from him. It is Miriam's refusal to allow him to regress to the Nirvana, the paradisal state of the infant, her insistence that he recognize her, that fills him with anguish."

As though to warn us against accepting Paul's responses and interpretations, Lawrence inserts in the middle of the crucial chapter, "Strife in Love," a long, vigorous, attractive, and surprising scene where the father is shown totally in command of the household, on a Friday evening, when the miners make their reckoning in Morel's house. Complaining with warm, vigorous dialect about the cold room, as he emerges from his bath, Morel draws even his wife into laughter and reminiscent admiration:

> Morel looked down ruefully at his sides.
> "Me!" he exclaimed. "I'm nowt b'r a skinned rabbit. My bones fair juts out on me."
> "I should like to know where," retorted his wife.
> "Iv'ry-wheer! I'm nobbut a sack o' faggots."
> Mrs. Morel laughed. He had still a wonderfully young body, muscular, without any fat. His skin was smooth and clear. It might have been the body of a man of twenty-eight, except that there were, perhaps, too many blue scars, like tattoo-marks, where the coal-dust remained under the skin, and that his chest was too hairy. But he put his hand on his sides ruefully. It was his fixed belief that, because he did not get fat, he was as thin as a starved rat.
> Paul looked at his father's thick, brownish hands all scarred, with broken nails, rubbing the fine smoothness of his sides, and the incongruity struck him. It seemed strange they were the same flesh.
> "I suppose," he said to his father, "you had a good figure once."
> "Eh!" exclaimed the miner, glancing round, startled and timid, like a child.
> "He had," exclaimed Mrs. Morel, "if he didn't hurtle

himself up as if he was trying to get in the smallest space he could."

"Me!" exclaimed Morel—"me a good figure! I wor niver much more n'r a skeleton."

"Man!" cried his wife, "don't be such a pulamiter!"

"'Strewth!" he said. "Tha's niver knowed me but what I looked as if I wor goin' off in a rapid decline."

She sat and laughed.

"You've had a constitution like iron," she said; "and never a man had a better start, if it was body that counted. You should have seen him as a young man," she cried suddenly to Paul, drawing herself up to imitate her husband's once handsome bearing.

Morel watched her shyly. He saw again the passion she had had for him. It blazed upon her for a moment. He was shy, rather scared, and humble. Yet again he felt his old glow. And then immediately he felt the ruin he had made during these years. He wanted to bustle about, to run away from it.

Paul is the "outsider" here, the one who does not enter into the family warmth, as we have seen a few lines earlier from his cold comment on his father's vigorous exclamations ("Why is a door-knob deader than anything else?"), and as we see a little later from the way in which he turns "impatiently" from his books and pencil, after his father has asked him "humbly" to count up the money. And at the close of the episode he dismisses his father viciously: "It won't be long," he says to his mother. "You can have my money. Let him go to hell." Morel does not deserve this, we feel, after all the warmth and vigour of his action here. Paul is cruel to anyone who threatens his mother's dominion, however briefly.

This Miriam feels instinctively, a few minutes later, when she looks at the stencilled design that Paul has made for his mother:

"Ah, how beautiful!" she cried.

The spread cloth, with its wonderful reddish roses and dark green stems, all so simple, and somehow so wicked-looking, lay at her feet. She went on her knees before it, her dark curls dropping. He saw her crouched voluptuously before his work, and his heart beat quickly. Suddenly she looked up at him.

"Why does it seem cruel?" she asked.

"What?"

"There seems a feeling of cruelty about it," she said.

"It's jolly good, whether or not," he replied, folding up his work with a lover's hands.

He has also made a "smaller piece" for Miriam; but when he sees her fingering the work "with trembling hands" he can only turn with embarrassment to tend the bread in the oven, and when she looks up at him "with her dark eyes one flame of love" he can only laugh "uncomfortably" and begin to talk "about the design." "All his passion, all his wild blood, went into this intercourse with her, when he talked and conceived his work. She brought forth to him his imaginations. She did not understand, any more than a woman understands when she conceives a child in her womb. But this was life for her and for him." But, as the imagery of conception ironically implies, such talk is not all of life for either of them.

Immediately after this, the physical scuffle and flirtation with Beatrice shows another need, which Miriam recognizes and would like to satisfy: "His thick hair was tumbled over his forehead. Why might she not push it back for him, and remove the marks of Beatrice's comb? Why might she not press his body with her two hands? It looked so firm, and every whit living. And he would let other girls, why not her?" A moment later, as usual, Paul tries to "abstract" their relationship into a French lesson, only to find that her French diary is "mostly a love-letter" to him:

"Look," he said quietly, "the past participle conjugated with *avoir* agrees with the direct object when it precedes."

She bent forward, trying to see and to understand. Her free, fine curls tickled his face. He started as if they had been red hot, shuddering. He saw her peering forward at the page, her red lips parted piteously, the black hair springing in fine strands across her tawny, ruddy cheek. She was coloured like a pomegranate for richness. His breath came short as he watched her. Suddenly she looked up at him. Her dark eyes were naked with their love, afraid, and yearning. His eyes, too, were dark, and they hurt her. They seemed to master her. She lost all her self-control, was exposed in fear. And he knew, before he could kiss her, he must drive something out of himself.

And a touch of hate for her crept back again into his heart.
He returned to her exercise.

Miriam does not bear the slightest blame for the failure of this relationship: she is "like a pomegranate for richness," like the bride in the Song of Solomon; she combines a pure beauty of sensuous appeal with all the soul that Paul the artist needs for his further development. And like that bride she is not passive, she tries to draw Paul out of his imprisonment, tries to draw his attention towards the wild beauty of "the yellow, bursten flowers." His response is to level at her the most cruel of all his desperate charges:

"Aren't they magnificent?" she murmured.
"Magnificent! it's a bit thick—they're pretty!"
She bowed again to her flowers at his censure of her praise. He watched her crouching, sipping the flowers with fervid kisses.
"Why must you always be fondling things!" he said irritably.
"But I love to touch them," she replied, hurt.
"Can you never like things without clutching them as if you wanted to pull the heart out of them? Why don't you have a bit more restraint, or reserve, or something?"
She looked up at him full of pain, then continued slowly to stroke her lips against a ruffled flower. Their scent, as she smelled it, was so much kinder than he; it almost made her cry.
"You wheedle the soul out of things," he said. "I would never wheedle—at any rate, I'd go straight."
He scarcely knew what he was saying. These things came from him mechanically. She looked at him. His body seemed one weapon, firm and hard against her.
"You're always begging things to love you," he said, "as if you were a beggar for love. Even the flowers, you have to fawn on them—"
Rhythmically, Miriam was swaying and stroking the flower with her mouth, inhaling the scent which ever after made her shudder as it came to her nostrils.
"You don't want to love—your eternal and abnormal craving is to be loved. You aren't positive, you're negative.

You absorb, absorb, as if you must fill yourself up with love, because you've got a shortage somewhere."

She was stunned by his cruelty, and did not hear. He had not the faintest notion of what he was saying. It was as if his fretted, tortured soul, run hot by thwarted passion, jetted off these sayings like sparks from electricity.

The shortage is in Paul; and she fondles the flowers so warmly because they offer solace from his ruthless rejection of her natural being. Her closeness to flowers throughout the book shows her as an innocent Persephone who needs only to be carried away by the power that Paul might possess if he were a whole man. But he is not. He is a child, with a child's limited outlook. His mother's influence has reduced all other human beings to unreality. This the narrator makes plain in one of his rare moments of illumination:

> He had come back to his mother. Hers was the strongest tie in his life. When he thought round, Miriam shrank away. There was a vague, unreal feel about her. And nobody else mattered. There was one place in the world that stood solid and did not melt into unreality: the place where his mother was. Everybody else could grow shadowy, almost non-existent to him, but she could not. It was as if the pivot and pole of his life, from which he could not escape, was his mother.

So then for Paul the warm reality of Miriam must fade away into spirituality and soulfulness, and she must suffer the cruel accusation summed up in the falsely composed letter that he writes at the end of the chapter, "Defeat of Miriam"—a letter of stilted, inflated rhetoric, false in every way:

> May I speak of our old, worn love, this last time. It, too, is changing, is it not? Say, has not the body of that love died, and left you its invulnerable soul? You see, I can give you a spirit love, I have given it you this long, long time; but not embodied passion. See, you are a nun. I have given you what I would give a holy nun—as a mystic monk to a mystic nun. Surely you esteem it best. Yet you regret— no, have regretted—the other. In all our relations no body enters. I do not talk to you through the senses—rather

through the spirit. That is why we cannot love in the common sense. Ours is not an everyday affection. As yet we
are mortal, and to live side by side with one another would
be dreadful, for somehow with you I cannot long be trivial, and, you know, to be always beyond this mortal state
would be to lose it. If people marry, they must live together as affectionate humans, who may be common-place
with each other without feeling awkward—not as two
souls. So I feel it.

So she feels it too, and the hopeless rejection of her true character
gives a death-blow to her inner vitality. " 'You are a nun—you are a
nun.' The words went into her heart again and again. Nothing he
ever had said had gone into her so deeply, fixedly, like a mortal
wound."

After such a wound, his later effort to carry on sexual relations
with her is bound to be a failure. She tries, as she always has tried,
but her inner life is ebbing. This is not the marriage that she yearns
for, not the union that he needs. Paul hardly knows that she is there,
as a person; indeed he does not want to know her as a human being.
"He had always, almost wilfully, to put her out of count, and act
from the brute strength of his own feelings." The title of the chapter,
"The Test on Miriam," is bitterly ironic, for what the chapter presents is the test on Paul's ability to free himself from the imprisonment which he feels, but does not understand. This is clear from
Paul's stream of consciousness at the very outset of the chapter:
"There was some obstacle; and what was the obstacle? It lay in the
physical bondage. He shrank from the physical contact. But why?
With her he felt bound up inside himself. He could not go out to
her." His only refuge is to turn towards a sort of mindless evasion of
his torments, a rejection of his own humanity:

He courted her now like a lover. Often, when he grew hot,
she put his face from her, held it between her hands, and
looked in his eyes. He could not meet her gaze. Her dark
eyes, full of love, earnest and searching, made him turn
away. Not for an instant would she let him forget. Back
again he had to torture himself into a sense of his responsibility and hers. Never any relaxing, never any leaving
himself to the great hunger and impersonality of passion;
he must be brought back to a deliberate, reflective crea-

ture. As if from a swoon of passion she called him back to the littleness, the personal relationship.

So Paul, near the end of this chapter, is reduced to pitiful, even contemptible, littleness. Miriam, in her violent despair, at last cries out the essential truth: "It has been one long battle between us—you fighting away from me." His response is shock and utter amazement: in his self-absorption he has never even begun to see it from her point of view. And he turns at once towards a painful series of self-justifications, throwing the blame on her: "He was full of a feeling that she had deceived him. She had despised him when he thought she worshipped him. She had let him say wrong things, and had not contradicted him. She had let him fight alone. . . . She had not played fair." Yet at the very end of the chapter, the bitter truth of what he has done to her emerges poignantly out of self-deception:

> "She never thought she'd have me, mother, not from the first, and so she's not disappointed."
> "I'm afraid," said his mother, "she doesn't give up hopes of you yet."
> "No," he said, "perhaps not."
> "You'll find it's better to have done," she said.
> "*I* don't know," he said desperately.
> "Well, leave her alone," replied his mother.
> So he left her, and she was alone. Very few people cared for her, and she for very few people. She remained alone with herself, waiting.

The Vital Self

Calvin Bedient

Nineteenth-century English novelists submitted, on the whole, to the dry world shrinkage of positivism. Their Christianity, where it obtained, was likely to be the echo, not the genuine cry, of faith. Jane Austen, Thackeray, Dickens, George Eliot, Meredith, Hardy—all relinquished the eternal in an attempt to take hold of the temporal; all were empiricists of human life. By mid-century the metaphysical hunger and ferment of the Romantics had all but disappeared. No wonder G. K. Chesterton found it necessary to complain, in 1905, that "everything matters—except everything." "The modern idea," Chesterton wrote in *Heretics,* "is that cosmic truth is so unimportant that it cannot matter what anyone says." By 1905, however, Shaw's *Man and Superman* had already been written, and Forster's explorations into a "terrible" and "mysterious" reality were under way: the Romantic appetite for the infiniteness of the cosmos was at that very moment being reborn. In Lawrence, Forster, and Virginia Woolf, in Yeats and Shaw, British literature was once again to open itself to wonder, to let in the stars.

It was in Lawrence's work above all that the eternal made inroads into the temporal, tearing up nineteenth-century skepticism and nearly tearing up the novels as well. No one else could approach Lawrence, in those early, metaphysically anarchic decades of the century, in the vigor and drama and urgency of his belief. Here was a

From *Architects of the Self.* © 1972 by the Regents of the University of California. University of California Press, 1972.

prophet, not out of the pages of history, but, of all things, in the
Café Royal, in Taos, in Oaxaca—a prophet very much in the flesh.
He did not belong, and he was not understood. Yet nothing could
shake his certainty and his mission. Almost alone in this century,
Lawrence enjoyed the forgotten luxury, and labored under the re-
sponsibility, of a metaphysical conviction.

It is curious how Lawrence's critics have held back from grant-
ing him his great fundamental certainty. Bewildered, perhaps, by the
secondary inconsistencies so rife in his work, by the absolute tone of
each partial statement—perhaps driven, too, by the notion that they
are "saving" Lawrence's art from ideas—they tend to see him as
lacking, in William Troy's words, "some cohesive view of the universe wholly absorbed in the personality" and to regard his works as
"records of the successive steps taken by his mind in the effort to
discover for himself some such view." The truth, however, is that
there was nothing but coherence for Lawrence. When Lawrence
said, for example, that "everything lies in *being,*" he spoke sincerely,
religiously, categorically. It was intuition, however, not intellectual
argument, that told him this was so. And, cohesive in itself, his intuition cast a philosophical shadow that was also to prove cohesive,
for all the broken appearance it took on from the changing planes of
Lawrence's mind. What sets Lawrence's work apart from that of his
great contemporaries, what makes it so strange and yet so compelling, is precisely its anachronistic passion and certitude, the way
Lawrence was immersed in it, breathing it like an atmosphere. If
there is anything "successive" in his work, it is his effort to unfold
an intuitive assurance already known, to lay it *finally* bare, and to
capture the satisfactions that seemed to be inherent in it.

What has yet to be noted is how Lawrence's metaphysic sprang
from and, indeed, *was* his experience—and also how it answered to
poignant psychological needs. Here was a man who believed—un-
accountably, it seemed—that there is in the universe a "principle towards which man turns religiously—a *life* of the universe itself."
And yet instead of appearing to be toying with metaphysics, he
seemed, on the contrary, to be burning with faith. His world-uniting
and world-revering belief glowed in everything he wrote, and constituted his mission. He spoke, not at a venture, but from the pulpit
of a certitude. How does a man come upon so much conviction?
Surely not at the behest of intellect. We must, I think, discount
Troy's opinion that it was "undoubtedly" in reaction "against the

scientific rationalism of the later nineteenth century" that Lawrence "plunged himself into the most abject nature-mysticism." The mind cannot do so much. Lawrence reacted, certainly, against scientific rationalism; but he reacted because of his mysticism, not into it. Lawrence's mysticism was a natural—or, as one prefers, an unnatural—involuntary growth. "It is not really helpful," Troy writes, "to be told by psychoanalysts that he suffered from one or another malady." On the contrary, Lawrence cannot be understood apart from his maladies. "Physical belief" of the kind that drove him can spring, like a geyser, only from subterranean pressures. And in Lawrence "physical belief" was, it would seem, the same as mystical belief. It is safe to guess—and, as we shall see, the records confirm—that something in Lawrence's notoriously strained filial experience, in combination with his exquisitely fluid sensibility, gave rise in him to a propensity to mysticism—to that whole world of "marvelous" feeling that would later crystallize into his rainbow-sensuous yet profoundly metaphysical world view. And thus it happens that to find the union of the man and his faith we would do well to look, not to his intellectual history, but to the point where his emotion finally bursts into the fire of his thought.

It is in *Sons and Lovers,* as I read it, that this conflagration first occurs. The book affords the rare opportunity of observing the genesis of an aesthetic metaphysical vision. And this genesis is not only of keen psychological interest in itself; it also provides a key to Lawrence's later development.

Alfred Kazin nearly puts his hand on this key when—in his fine introduction to the Modern Library edition of the novel—he notes that Lawrence's motive as a writer was his attempt to re-create "the mutual sympathy he had experienced with his mother." Kazin, however, goes awry when he adds that this "ecstasy . . . never congealed into a single . . . idol or belief." In fact, it congealed into a metaphysic that was to become the mainstay of Lawrence's fiction. After *Sons and Lovers,* especially, the universe Lawrence lived in, and wrote in so beautifully, was but the glowing flesh or, at worst, the eternally renewed promise of the mystical self-dispersal that Lawrence had known with his mother. Both belief and idol, it was a universe of apotheosized feeling.

This burgeoning of psychology into metaphysics is the hidden drama of *Sons and Lovers.* If it is easy to miss, the reason is that the oedipal drama, with its crackling tensions and dilemmas, is the foreground in a novel that is, after all, almost entirely foreground. Consisting, as it does, of a few scattered paragraphs, the metaphysic of *Sons and Lovers* might seem merely incidental—musings in the intervals of the oedipal conflict. Indeed, Lawrence presents it as scarcely more than incidental. In reality, however, it constitutes, not a digression from the psychological dilemma, but precisely its solution—insofar, that is, as it was to admit of one.

On the oedipal plane itself we find an impasse, a crippling relationship too powerful to overcome. Paul Morel cannot desire where he loves; and he cannot love where he desires. Body and soul will not conjoin. His soul is bonded to his mother's, irrevocably; his body, however, "mad with restlessness," urges him "towards something else." Yet with neither the refined and thoughtful Miriam nor the robust and sensual Clara does Paul manage to free himself from his mother. He only appears to travel from her, as a man in a snowstorm, wandering in a circle, only supposes he is leaving the scene of his despair.

Sensing Paul's misery, Mrs. Morel grows tired and takes ill; and both Paul and his mother hope, even as they fear, that her death will free him at last to "really love another woman." His life has been "like a circle where life turned back on itself"—his mother "bore him, loved him, kept him, and his love turned back into her." But Mrs. Morel's death fails to break the circle: "His soul could not leave her, wherever she was. Now she was gone abroad into the night, and he was with her still." So we learn from the last page of the book.

Even though dead, Mrs. Morel holds Paul "up, himself." His identity, then, is somehow one with hers. She, however, has gone "abroad in the night"; hence it is with the vast night, much as it terrifies him, that Paul must now begin to feel connected. His mother has passed into the world; will not the world now "be" his mother? "So instead of a release and a deliverance from bondage, the bondage was glorified and made absolute": thus, shrewdly, Jessie Chambers, the original of the Miriam of the novel. "Lawrence handed his mother the laurels of victory," she added. Indeed he did; but it was on the "living" universe that he placed the laurels. His bond with his mother came to be his bond with time and space and with whatever might lie "beyond."

As Daniel Weiss, Frank O'Connor, and others have shown, Freudian theory accounts for a good deal of Paul's story. Indeed, Freud's "The Most Prevalent Form of Degradation in Erotic Life" reads almost like a direct comment on Lawrence's brave and stunning book. And doubtless Lawrence's own connection with his mother, like Paul's, could not easily have been more "oedipal" than it was; it was a classic case. Yet Freudian theory does not explain enough. It leaves untouched the strength of Paul's connection with his mother, the iron in it, and the ease with which it passes, at her death, and indeed (as we shall see) before it, into a mystical worship of the world.

Lawrence's bond with his mother was—no other word—mystical. And it was this, I believe, that made it the unalterable and magically strengthening bond that it was. It was this that made it the seed of a mystical vitalism. Lawrence described this aspect of the relationship in a letter sent to Rachel Annand Taylor in December 1910:

> We knew each other by instinct. She said to my aunt— about me:
>
> "But it has been different with him. He has seemed to be part of me."—And that is the real case. We have been like one, so sensitive to each other that we never needed words. It has been rather terrible and has made me, in some respects, abnormal.
>
> I think this *peculiar fusion of soul* . . . never comes twice in a life-time—*it doesn't seem natural.* When it comes it seems to distribute one's consciousness far abroad from oneself, and one understands! I think no one has got "Understanding" except through love [my italics].

Lawrence concluded: "Nobody can have the soul of me. My mother has had it, and nobody can have it again. Nobody can come into my very self again, and breathe me like an atmosphere."

This letter, so bleak and absolute, has the uncompromising accents of truth. And surely what it reveals is that, whatever else it may have been, Lawrence's bond with his mother was mystical: a shaft into revelation, a numinous enlargement of self. So absolute was it that, Lawrence believed, there could be no going beyond it. Nor could merely personal or, for that matter, sexual relationships seem anything but desolation by comparison. No wonder Paul cannot be satisfied with Miriam or Clara, that he is always wanting "something else." And no wonder his mother seems to him the "pivot" of everything: the "one place in the world that . . . did not melt into unreality." There in the past, so Lawrence must always have felt, was the farthest reach that his soul could go. Why should he then try to break out of the "circle"?

The true problem, rather, was to bring his body into it. This he could not do, of course, so long as his mother was the obvious "pivot" of his soul. And hence Paul is right to try to free himself through sexual intercourse with other women. But it is not other women who then seem to be the new "reality" with which his soul is fused. It is the world. "The highest of all was to melt out into the darkness and sway there, identified with the great Being," Paul feels after intercourse with Miriam. And as for intercourse with Clara: "They had met and included in their meeting the thrust of the manifold grass stems, the cry of the peewit, the wheel of the stars." Together they "know the tremendous living food which carried them always, gave them rest within themselves." So Clara has reason to complain that she is not really there for Paul. None of Lawrence's heroes ever "really loves a woman." Though all passionate lovers, it is the Infinite that they love, "the great Being." They go to a woman as metal goes into a furnace, for a "melting out."

So it was that, seeking to escape his "circle" with his mother through sexual relations, Lawrence found himself in a still greater circle, a circle as large as the world. Trying to leave the filial circle through eroticism, he only expanded and eroticized it. Sex with its tendency to dissolve the ego, to merge the mind with the blood, freed him from any limited personal attachment and, in the words of his letter to Mrs. Taylor, distributed his "consciousness far abroad." In sexual intercourse Lawrence seems to have found himself, not really free from his mother, but precisely where his relation with her had always put him—at the heart of "Understanding." As if by a homing instinct, his body found its way at last, without conscious guilt, into that "peculiar fusion" that his soul had so long enjoyed. And so it was that Lawrence became the messiah of sexual intercourse, of a "wholeness" known only in the blood.

What sexual congress brought into view for Lawrence was not a bodiless realm of the soul but precisely the world as the body of the soul: the world as the tremendous living flood that gives the soul rest within itself. In such a *founded* carnal creation, where matter is so necessary to spirit, the body became as real to Lawrence as the soul—as centered and as luminously radiant. And not only did the expanded circle of the soul make room for the body; it was dependent upon the body, which served as its eye or, better, as the hand that felt it. So it was that the long-estranged sensual and spiritual currents in Lawrence finally flowed together. In sexual intercourse, he became whole. At the same instant, he merged with the Whole. Hence the apparent contradiction in Lawrence's later insistence on being "single" and "integral" and, on the other hand, on "melting out." For Lawrence, at least in sexual congress, these two states were one.

Why does Lawrence not make more of this "solution" to his problem in *Sons and Lovers?* The reason, I think, is that he is not yet conscious of it as one. When he was to become conscious of it, he would make more of it than it could easily bear. He would generalize it as a solution for the miseries of all men. And he would pretend or hope that it would yield a more lasting satisfaction than it could, dependent as it was upon passing physical sensation. But meanwhile he merely accepts it as a datum of his experience; he "makes" nothing of it. He enjoys it as a solution before he recognizes it as one. Hence the total absence of surprise in his hero Paul, who suddenly finds himself, in sexual congress, in the midst of a "great Being" without the least sign of astonishment. It is as if he were simply entering his own living room. And, indeed, with Lawrence was this not in a sense the case? The large circle of the great Being is, after all, identical in essence with the filial one; however far the first reaches out to the stars, a Nottinghamshire parlor once accommodated it. The attributes that (according to Mircea Eliade) distinguish the sacred—namely power, reality, being, the founded, and permanence—were, for Lawrence, common to both his mother and the great Being. Lawrence was to be "born" from each, loved by each, kept by each, and his soul was to turn back to find its source in each. Sexual intercourse thus awakened in him only a familiar intuition. So it is that the bud of the Absolute opens in *Sons and Lovers* without surprise or remark.

If Lawrence's bond with his mother was in one sense inescapable, in another it merely prepared the way for what was to become the great bond of his life and the great theme of his work: his sympathy with the world. The metaphysic so casually cast up in *Sons and Lovers* will be elaborated and become all-pervading in the books to follow. On the other hand, the oedipal dilemma as such will simply disappear, a "solution" to it having been found.

Perhaps only in one way did Lawrence's memory of his mother color the concept of Being that otherwise became detached from her.

Whenever her death, his own isolation, struck him afresh, his sense of Being was invaded by shadow: the "night" then became more an invitation to death than an assurance that his mother held him up even from there. His notion of Being was thus to oscillate between activity and stillness, flaming life and shadowy death. Now it was a "tremendous living flood"; now the place to enter a "death sleep." As Lawrence said in his poem "At a Loose End," his mother's death threw "a shadow inviolate" into his own "flame of living." When the flame was low, the shadow loomed forth and became the night.

Even apart from this morbid element, Lawrence's erotic experience of Being was never to prove a true redemption. His intuition of a universal life perhaps stitched and sustained him but, as was suggested, could not satisfy him. If it afforded deep security and peace, it did so only on occasion; there was always the need to begin the quest again. Hence the restlessness, the repeated "rebirths," in Lawrence's heroes and heroines. "Being," after all, does not make a satisfactory lover; hard to find, it is still harder to hold on to. Lawrence liked to believe that mysticism could be a permanent state of the soul; but judging from his protagonists, Lawrence must often have found himself waiting, like an empty vessel, to be filled.

Regardless of this, Lawrence's feeling that a "great Being" supported his body and soul was one of the strongest ever to give birth to art. And what rich observation, what passionate conceptions, it sponsored. It is impossible altogether to regret the controlling role of mystical intuition in Lawrence's books. And all the more is this so when one realizes that, far from being an intellectual construction, it was the mainspring of his being: the one thing that gave him the mission to write and the one thing besides that permitted him to be whole.

Speaking of Paul Morel: Voice, Unity, and Meaning in *Sons and Lovers*

Daniel R. Schwarz

Beginning with the earliest reviews of *Sons and Lovers*, Lawrence has been indicted for his "inability to efface himself" and for giving us a "narrative [that] reads like an autobiography." Later, Mark Schorer's provocative remarks about the confusion between Lawrence's "intention and performance" sharply focused critical attention upon the crucial relationship between voice and form in *Sons and Lovers*. Schorer argued that *Sons and Lovers* should be considered a "technical failure" whose "artistic coherence" has been destroyed by its inconsistencies. Specifically, he observed "the contradiction between Lawrence's explicit characterizations of the mother and father and his tonal evaluations of them"; he also remarked upon the novel's efforts both to "condemn" and "justify" the mother and both to expose and rationalize Paul's failures.

Schorer's complaint about the novel's aesthetic unity reflects both his discomfort with a novel that implies conflicting and contradictory values, and his belief that if a reader has to engage in judging the reliability and perspicacity of a technically omniscient third person speaker, the integrity of the novel is necessarily disturbed. In this essay I shall argue that: (1) the discrepancies between the narrator's interpretations and ours create a tension that becomes an intrinsic part of the novel's form; (2) the fluctuating and complex relationship between the narrator and his major characters enables the reader to

From *Studies in the Novel* 8, no. 3 (Fall 1976). © 1976 by North Texas State University.

participate in the agonizing but wonderfully exciting *aesthetic* process by which an author tries to give shape and unity to his recent past; and (3) the failure of Lawrence to sort out the blame, to neatly "master" his materials, is a major reason for the novel's subtlety and complexity.

Louis L. Martz has convincingly refuted Schorer. Arguing for the efficacy of Lawrence's technique in chapters 7 ("Lad-and-Girl Love") through 11 ("The Test on Miriam"), he writes:

> The point of view adopted is that of Paul; but since confusion, self-deception, and desperate self-justification are essential to that point of view, we can never tell, from the stream of consciousness alone, where the real truth lies. But we can tell it from the action; we can tell it by seeking out the portrait of Miriam that lies beneath the overpainted commentary of the Paul-narrator. This technique of painting and overpainting produces a strange and unique tension in this part of the novel.

Though Martz's fine essay considerably furthers the discussion of the aesthetic unity of *Sons and Lovers,* I should like to take issue with him on several counts: (1) I do not believe Lawrence "resumes" "the method of the objective narrator" in chapters 12 ("Passion") through 15 ("Derelict"), and I do not perceive a tonal change in the narrator's voice in these later chapters of part 2. (2) I do not agree that the narrator in part 1 is "working with firm control, [setting] forth the facts objectively." (3) I think Martz's insistence on seeing a "growth in [Paul's] self-knowledge" deflects him into a reading of the ending that blurs the negative implications of the final paragraphs. (4) I feel that his term "overpainting" ignores the temporal nature of the reader's perception of a work of fiction. Although a reader's impressions are continually qualified or even displaced by subsequent narrative commentary or dramatized scenes, two contrasting impressions do not really exist in the reader's mind simultaneously like a negative that has been double exposed.

Lawrence's struggle to come to terms with his own experience is revealed in the novel's conflict between narrative incident and narrator commentary. This conflict reflects Lawrence's continuing reevaluation of his experience as he rewrote *Sons and Lovers* at a time when he was torn between the desire to be true to the sacred memory of his mother and to respond to the views of first Jessie Chambers and later Frieda. To come to terms with his autobiographical material, Lawrence tries to divide himself into two separate characters: Paul and the narrator. Paul, a former self and the embodiment of his past, is a subjective creation; Lawrence immerses Paul in a narrative that mimes crucial events of his own life, but does not ask Paul to judge himself scrupulously. That task is left to the narrator, the embodiment of the present self who is supposed to be an objective figure charged with evaluating and measuring Lawrence's former self and tracing his linear development. But this dichotomy breaks down as Lawrence's objective self becomes empathetic to his former self, Paul Morel. Because Lawrence is not emotionally removed from the narrated experience, his superego has not grown sufficiently beyond the experience to evaluate and control his own mother-love. (In a December 1910 letter written while his mother was dying, Lawrence had said of the relationship with his mother: "We have loved each other, almost with a husband and wife love, as well as filial and maternal.") That his narrator's consciousness is incompletely developed and very much in the process of becoming is appropriate for a novel in which the protagonist's aesthetic rejects "the stiffness of shape" for the "shimmeriness" inside.

The narrator is an apologist for Mrs. Morel and an adversary of Miriam. He takes distinctly different stances toward similar behavior in the two women. If it is proper for Paul to resist having his "soul" possessed by Miriam, why is the narrator rather tolerant of Mrs. Morel's "root[ing]" her life in Paul and becoming "the pivot and pole of his life, from which he could not escape"? Anxious to justify Mrs. Morel's behavior, the narrator provides half-convincing excuses in which he desperately wishes to believe.

The narrator perceives Mrs. Morel's insistent claims upon Paul within individual scenes, but he is unwilling to recognize the significance of the evolving pattern. He is aware how Mrs. Morel has substituted her sons for her husband, but refuses to acknowledge how individually organic moments with his mother, in which they share attitudes, ideas, and epiphanies of nature's beauty, add up to a perverse pattern. Nor does he acknowledge that Mrs. Morel's smothering and stifling maternity is often conscious, volitional, and willful. In the final scene in part 1, the narrator refuses to recognize the implications of what is occurring when Mrs. Morel transfers her affections from the recently deceased William to Paul, while the latter is suffering from pneumonia. The narrator empathizes with both

Paul and his mother and renders the scene without irony or detachment:

> "I s'll die, mother!" he cried, heaving for breath on the pillow.
> She lifted him up, crying in a small voice:
> "Oh, my son—my son!"
> That brought him to. He realised her. His whole will rose up and arrested him. He put his head on her breast, and took ease of her for love. . . .
> The two knitted together in perfect intimacy. Mrs. Morel's life now rooted itself in Paul.

Their mutual passion is restorative for both of them. But this apparently perfect moment of intimacy forges a fateful link that severely impedes Paul's sexual and emotional growth. Subsequent events make clear to the reader that it is Mrs. Morel's complicity in the oedipal love—her willingness to fuse herself to him—that blights Paul's maturation. But does the narrator acknowledge that this fusion (a concept which Lawrence disfavorably contrasts in *The Study of Thomas Hardy* with the "Two-in-One") of two lives is potentially destructive? If there seems to be a hint of ambivalence in the words "rooted" and "knitted," this is extinguished by the insistence that the new relationship is restorative for both of them. As he recalls this scene, Lawrence's speaker cherishes rather than criticizes the intimacy between his younger self and his mother.

Yet Lawrence undoubtedly meant to create a speaker who, while sympathetic toward Paul, could detach himself enough from Paul's oedipal love so as to be able to show the reader more about the protagonist than Paul knew about himself. In the novel's first part, Lawrence tries with some success to establish a discrepancy between the narrator's perspective and Paul's and demonstrates that Lawrence wishes to separate himself from Paul. But the autobiographical material of *Sons and Lovers* resisted the convention of omniscient narration in which Lawrence conceived it. When he evolves Paul's responses to nature and sex, when he seeks to translate the silence of Paul's unconscious into nondiscursive rhythms and images, Lawrence is completely empathetic toward Paul and the narrative distance breaks down completely. The objective voice, the evaluative superego with his gently ironic view of Lawrence's younger self, is displaced by the urgent voice of the fates seeking to transport the reader into a sensual, vitalistic rapport with the young man who is finally discovering his long repressed passional self. For example, notice the texture of the passage in which Lawrence renders Paul's and Clara's most successful sexual consummation, the one that takes place in the fields along the canal:

> All the while the peewits were screaming in the field. When he came to, he wondered what was near his eyes, curving and strong with life in the dark, and what voice it was speaking. Then he realised it was the grass, and the peewit was calling. The warmth was Clara's breathing heaving. He lifted his head, and looked into her eyes. They were dark and shining and strange, life wild at the source staring into his life, stranger to him, yet meeting him; and he put his face down on her throat, afraid. What was she? A strong, strange, wild life, that breathed with his in the darkness through this hour. It was all so much bigger than themselves that he was hushed. They had met, and included in their meeting the thrust of the manifold grass stems, the cry of the peewit, the wheel of the stars.

In such sexual and passionate moments, Lawrence is intruding into the silence of unconscious physiological experience and inviting the reader to participate directly in the sensual life of his characters. His metaphors seek to transform the space in which the sexual act or passionate moment occurs into a place where the texture of life is sensuous, physical, instinctive, and biological and where cognitive life is absent. Such metaphors, rather than creating objective correlatives, are lyrical explosions whose rhythms and images are supposed to immediately engage the reader's libidinous self without the intervening cognitive process by which a reader usually transforms a narrative episode into signification. A sentence such as "They had met, and included in their meeting the thrust of the manifold grass stems, the cry of the peewit, the wheel of the stars" implies that during the sexual act the power of the participants' libidinous energy displaces the diurnal world in which they dwell and makes their world coterminous and spatially equivalent with the cosmos; in a word, microcosm becomes macrocosm. When it works as I believe it does here, Lawrence's style *becomes* his argument. Sexual intercourse enables the participants to become part of the natural world and the energy that breathes through it; in Blakean terms, it restores if only temporarily the lapsed soul to Beulah.

II

While acknowledging the complexity of part 2, Martz calls part 1 "a triumph of narration in the old Victorian style" of objective omniscient narration. But the fluctuating perspective of the first chapters is rather more complex than he allows. Desiring to render Mr. Morel with objectivity and to acknowledge his vitality, the narrator depicts him making his fuses, fixing his breakfast, and, especially, relishing his masculine holidays. The narrator does show how Mrs. Morel isolates Morel from his own children, and even briefly adopts a perspective sympathetic to Morel when analyzing the deterioration of the marriage. On rare occasions, the narrator depicts the frustrations of *both* ill-matched partners. When Morel cuts William's hair, the narrator catches the pathology of his wife's rage: "I could kill you, I could!" Yet his sympathy is with Mrs. Morel. Basically, the narrator empathizes with her desire for a sanctuary from "poverty," "ugliness," and "meanness," and he fails to stress—as the reader soon learns from dramatized scenes—that her dissatisfaction with her lot makes impossible a viable relationship with her husband. Mrs. Morel's "air of authority" and "rare warmth" give her primacy within her home and within the lives of her children. While acknowledging her inability to accept her husband, the narrator minimizes how her willful desire to establish to her children that she is better than her husband preempts his position in the family. As she gradually establishes her dominant position, *she* assumes the role of father.

The first chapter establishes the pattern of the novel. Mrs. Morel evaluates her husband and his companions according to arbitrary social and economic standards. Mrs. Morel has a compulsion to improve herself and her family. In a perverse way that neither she nor the narrator understands, she equates material and social progress with blessedness. Trying in turn to shape Morel, William, and Paul, she creates for each of them expectations that they cannot meet. Morel's *manners* distress her, but her continual search for a surrogate husband begins when she learns that he does not take pride in his economic independence. That he actually pays his mother's rent disturbs her as much or more than that he has lied. Just like her father she is proud of her "integrity," but integrity in a husband means something rather narrow to her: the ability to pay one's bills and to provide for one's wife. (She would not deign to take in mending like the other Bottoms' wives.) Morel's drinking is to her, above all, indicative of his economic and social irresponsibility which undermines her efforts to consider herself better than her neighbors. If ever Mrs. Morel indicts herself as niggling and petty, it is when she recalls: "[Morel] had bought no engagement ring at all, and she preferred William, who was not mean, if he were foolish." As she begins to allow William to play the role of surrogate husband, she unconsciously seeks to reduce her husband to a child; we recall how she mocks his efforts to run away after he had stealthily taken sixpence from her pocketbook. Meanwhile, as if she were a feudal "queen" she accepts "tribute" from William who "gave all his money to his mother." William is subconsciously compelled to choose for a sexual partner someone who is the complete opposite to his mother-lover whom he has unconsciously dedicated himself to serving chivalrically. Mrs. Morel needs to control, dominate, and subdue; yet one part of her despises her husband because he allows himself to be emasculated: "She sat trembling slightly, but her heart brimming with contempt. What would she do if he went to some other pit, obtained work, and got in with another woman? But she knew him too well—he couldn't. She was dead sure of him."

Unconsciously at first but later quite intentionally, she transfers her libidinous self—the nighttime self that in spite of her rationality and pragmatism responds to the sensuality of flowers and moonlight—to her children because she finds her husband's social, public self wanting. The first chapter shows how Mrs. Morel struggles between, on the one hand, the external norms that she has inherited from the Coppard tradition, and, on the other, her sensual and passionate potential. No matter how she would deny her biological self and renounce Morel, her libido expresses itself in her physical response to her husband and her narcissistic experience with flowers. As her orgasmic moment with the symbolically virginal lilies indicates (she "melts out" of herself into "a kind of swoon"), Mrs. Morel is no longer by the time chapter 1 ends completely dependent upon her husband to fulfill her sexual needs. (Whatever Lawrence's intention, I think that the scenes in which Mrs. Morel, Paul, Miriam, and even Clara have passionate intercourse with flowers must be regarded in part as a function of their sexual frustrations.)

If part 1 did have an objective narrator, would he not stress how Paul's class snobbery, self-righteousness, and ambition are shaped by the force of his mother's will? Mrs. Morel is obsessed with her sons' social and economic success because of her husband's failure to give her the vicarious recognition and economic status that she craves: "She felt . . . that where [Paul] determined to go he would get. . . . Now she had two sons in the world. She could think of two places, great centres of industry, and feel that she had put a man into each of them, that these men would work out what *she* wanted; they were derived from her, they were of her, and their works also would be hers." The narrator accepts Paul's view that his mother's "hardness" and defensive behavior are rather understandable in light of the disappointments she has endured. Explaining how she copes with her anxiety about sending a fourteen-year-old boy to work at a factory, where his health suffers from "darkness" and "lack of air," the narrator explains: "But she herself had had to put up with so much that she expected her children to take the same odds. They must go through with what came." Mrs. Morel is aggressive and even hostile to those with whom she has an economic relationship; one need only recall the waitress at Nottingham, the man who drives the carriage to the cottage that the family has rented, or even the man from whom she buys a decorated dish. While Paul's response to the mine is aesthetic, imaginative, and organic, hers is primarily economic. When Paul notices the beauty of the pits, she can only think of the economic significance, notwithstanding her prior observation that "the world is a wonderful place."

Once William indicates the extent of his attachment to Gipsy, Paul begins to replace him as Mrs. Morel's surrogate husband. When Morel breaks his leg, "in her heart of hearts, where the love should have burned, there was a blank." Even though she continues to have intermittent if infrequent feelings of affection for her husband, her attitude at this time gives special urgency to the imploring question that she asks Paul: "What do you want to be?" At the age of fourteen, he accepts without protest her charge that he make his way in the world, although the thought of taking a job seems like "bondage" to him and "[kills] all joy and even life." But in her determination that he succeed, Mrs. Morel is oblivious to his needs. Significantly her concern for Paul's success in the outer world corresponds to her gradual realization that William is betraying her trust and her love. The emphasis on Paul in chapter 5 ("Paul Launches into Life") alternates with brief but significant vignettes about William. Before Mrs. Morel sets off to Nottingham with Paul, "gay, like a sweetheart," she has begun to suspect that William, who sent her money only twice from London, is not fulfilling the acknowledged role of provider and the suppressed role of gallant knight that would make him a substitute for Morel.

Although at first Mrs. Morel seems physically and psychically weakened after William's death, she recuperates when Paul's illness gives her an opportunity to transfer her affections to the next son. As William's relationship with Gyp had developed in intensity and as William had ceased to pay her economic homage, she already had begun turning toward Paul: "Mrs. Morel clung now to Paul. . . . Still he stuck to his painting and still he stuck to his mother. Everything he did was for her. She waited for his coming home in the evening, and then she unburdened herself of all she had pondered, or of all that had occurred to her during the day. . . . The two shared lives." Perhaps in the choice of verbs ("clung," "stuck," "unburdened"), we can feel something of Lawrence's resentment as his narrator recalls how Paul was asked to play a role of surrogate husband that deprived him of much of adolescence. Since Mrs. Morel teaches her children by example to be dissatisfied with spouse and home, William's disastrous choice of someone completely unsuited to him and the very antithesis of the people he has known, as well as Paul's dissatisfaction with the women in his life, can be in part attributed to Mrs. Morel's influence. How devastating is the effect on the young adolescent of his mother's speaking of the family parlour as "a beastly cold, sunless hole."

Just like the mother in "The Rocking-Horse Winner" (1926), Mrs. Morel's economic discontent wrenches family relationships. Yet we see little to indicate that the Morels are ever so destitute that it interferes with their basic comfort. Mrs. Morel attributes almost magical significance to money. As in the later story, money becomes a virtual substitute for sperm. Money is the means by which Mrs. Morel accepts sexual fealty. Both her resentment of Gyp, and of Morel's male camaraderie and the concomitant drinking involves not only anger that money is being wasted, but sexual jealousy. Until his affair with Gyp, she takes special pride in William's salary. Money is a sanctioned sexual tribute that her sons may deliver without guilt on the part of giver or recipient. The narrator's voice has a touch of wonder and awe as he recounts how William becomes ill because he has delivered both his money and his actual sperm to Gipsy. Of course, to a considerable extent William is based on the actual history of Lawrence's brother Ernest. But within the fictive world William's sudden pneumonia and subsequent death have the parabolic, non-mimetic quality of Paul's death in "The Rocking-Horse Winner," as if he is being punished for some mysterious transgression involving the mother.

Beginning with chapter 4 ("The Young Life of Paul"), the structure of each chapter affirms the extent of Paul's bondage to his mother and the claustrophobic effect of these ties upon his emotional development. Characteristically, a chapter raises the hope of experience which will move Paul outward. But, gradually, Mrs. Morel's influence restricts and confines the possibility of new relationships and important self-discovery. Each movement outward is arrested by his obsession with his mother. For example, chapter 7, "Lad-and-Girl Love," begins with the promise of exorcising the intense but destructive passion between mother and son with which part 1 ended. Paul and Miriam are both excessively self-conscious but they gradually establish rapport. Throughout the chapter, Mrs. Morel's disapproval intervenes to block the natural development of his relationship with Miriam. This chapter's conclusion shows why "their intimacy was so abstract" and why he "suppressed into a shame" his sexual desire; his mother's rebuke for returning late punctuates a chapter in which his loyalty to his mother comes between Miriam and himself. At crucial moments, when he is tormented by his passion for his mother and tortured by his inability to respond sexually to Miriam or his mother, his repressed libidinous urges find an outlet in antagonism to Miriam: "He hated her, for she seemed in some way to make him despise himself. . . . He loved to think of his mother, and the other jolly people." (Of course, his mother is, with rare exception, a humorless figure.)

In the next chapter, "Strife in Love," the narrator shifts his focus on Miriam and Paul to show briefly how the mother's influence continues. When Paul wins the painting contest, her joy has a self-indulgent aspect as she takes these victories as self-vindication. "Paul was going to distinguish himself. . . . She was to see herself fulfilled. Not for nothing had been her struggle." The extent to which Mrs. Morel's perspective, which to the reader seems limited and self-serving, is given legitimacy and implicit endorsement by the narrator can be seen when the narrator anticipates Mrs. Morel's thought that Miriam "wants to absorb him" with the comment that "[Miriam] loved him absorbedly." Paul's reasons for hating Miriam are illogical, implausible, and revealing: "If Miriam caused his mother suffering then he hated her—and he easily hated her. Why did she make him feel as if he were uncertain of himself, insecure, an indefinite thing?" Later in the chapter, after he seems to have found an outlet for his libido in adolescent sex play with Beatrice, Mrs. Morel rebukes him for failing to care for the bread while Miriam was there. His response is to remind her of his age: "You're old, mother, and we're young." This is the catalyst for a quarrel which ends in Mrs. Morel's conclusive triumph over Miriam: their passionate incestuous embrace.

The narrator continually insists upon distinctions between Miriam and Paul, and between Miriam and Mrs. Morel, while the narrative shows that in many ways the Leivers family mirrors the Morels. If Miriam is a "maiden in bondage, her spirit dreaming in a land far away and magical," Paul is a lad in bondage to his mother. Considering the altercations and antipathy that divide the Morel family, it is astonishing that Paul criticizes the "jangle and discord in the Leivers family." That Paul is immediately attracted to the rather supercilious and patronizing Leivers family at all shows how he has been educated by Mrs. Morel's social pretensions. His attraction to someone whom he later suspects of wishing to dominate him and who imagines herself a "princess turned into a swine-girl" shows that he responds to those qualities that suggest his mother. That Miriam feels a need to "swathe" and "stifle" her four-year-old brother recalls vividly how Mrs. Morel passionately encloses her sons. The narrator gives a motive for Mrs. Morel's jealousy by implying, without ever providing dramatic corroboration, that Miriam wishes to mother Paul. "If she could be mistress of him in his weakness, take care of him, if he could depend on her, if she could, as it were, have him in her arms, how she would love him!" As Paul becomes dependent on Miriam for aesthetic stimulation and for bringing out his spiritual aspect, he almost gives her the status of his mother and creates competition between the two women within his psyche. On the other hand, there are substantial differences between the Leivers and Paul's own family. He is first attracted to Mrs. Leivers because she responds to the significance of an experience in other than economic terms. In contrast to his mother's expedience and pragmatism, the Leivers perceive spiritually and abstractly. Their effect on him is different: "They kindled him and made him glow to his work, whereas his mother's influence was to make him quietly determined, patient, dogged, unwearied."

Within the narrative, it often seems that Miriam represents the "shimmeriness" which is "the real living," while it is the mother who is the "shape" which "is a dead crust." If Paul talks about "shimmeriness," he does so in "abstract" speeches, while it is Miriam's "dark eyes alight with water that shakes with a stream of gold in the dark." When she yearns for him, he desires to kiss her in "abstract purity" and then he criticizes her for not "[realizing] the male he was." In "Strife in Love," while he is watching his mother's bread and teaching Miriam French, Miriam is described in terms that suggest the bride in Song of Songs ("She was coloured like a pomegranate for richness.") and only awaits Paul's sexual response to arouse her. "Her dark eyes were naked with their love, afraid, and yearning." But it is Paul who cannot respond: "He knew, before he could kiss her, he must drive something out of himself." As Paul stomps to the oven, Lawrence's narrator cannot help revealing how Paul has affected his vulnerable but complaisant friend: "Even the way he crouched before the oven hurt her. There seemed to be something cruel in it, something cruel in the swift way he pitched the bread out of the tins." Rather than allowing Miriam to complement his experience and enjoy her difference, he uses his mother's qualities as norms to judge the difference he discovers in Miriam: "Her intensity, which would leave no emotion on a normal plane, initiated the youth into a frenzy. . . . He was used to his mother's reserve. And on such occasions, he was thankful in his heart and soul that he had his mother, so *sane* and *wholesome*" (my italics).

The narrator's distinction between Miriam's desire to shape Paul and his mother's need to will his future often seems a distinction without a difference. Like Mrs. Morel, Miriam "gave him all her love and her faith" and wishes to "guard" the best of him from the pollution of the outside world. Deliberately mocking both Miriam's view of her sexual role and the hyperbolic conventions of platonic love to which (according to him) she subscribes, the narrator remarks: "Nay, the sky did not cherish the stars more surely and eternally than she would guard the good in the soul of Paul Morel." Using ironic religious language, the narrator presents Miriam's self-sacrifice as perverse: "Miriam [is] tortured . . . [because] he [is] utterly unfaithful to her." But Mrs. Morel is also a worshipper who

denies herself so that her godhead might flourish. She is tortured by
his need for a sexual partner. And she, too, transfers her sublimated
passion into religious paroxysm: She "prayed and prayed for him,
that he might not be wasted." Even more than Miriam's prayers, hers
derive from her compulsion to shape his life to her model, and to
live through his achievements. Mrs. Morel's prayer is the expression
of her will and hence, according to the values that pervade Lawrence's work, mechanistic and contrary to organic being. The reader
understands that prayer is a socially sanctioned means by which she
can direct her son's life. Intellectually Paul knows "that one should
feel inside oneself for right and wrong, and should have the patience
to gradually realise one's God." But because he has "realised" his
mother, his god—the individuating principle that makes each man
himself and enables him to tap his latent potential—eludes him. The
narrative dramatizes the tension between extrinsic standards inculcated by his mother and his inherent need to fulfill himself.

III

Our basic premise has been that Paul's inadequacies were unconsciously ignored and underplayed by the narrator, but that the dramatic events render a more complex vision of the human relationships that form the subject of *Sons and Lovers*. The preterite does not
guarantee objectivity. That Lawrence was still coming to terms with
the experience that forms the novel's raw material undoubtedly de-
flected him from objective analysis. The tension between the narrator's mythmaking and the greater objectivity of much of the dramatic action may be part of the hold that the novel exercises upon its
readers. We, as readers, participate in Lawrence's continuous and
often ineffectual struggles with his mother's influence and his oedipal
love. The concatenation of individual moments gives a different perspective to the scenes in which Paul and Miriam struggle with their
inhibitions and psychic problems. The narrator's persistent efforts to
attribute to Miriam insidious emotions that are not demonstrated
within the dramatic action finally raise doubts about the quality of
the narrator's analyses.

An example of how the narrative renders the complexities of the
issues despite the narrator's insistent defense of Paul occurs in the
early pages of "Defeat of Miriam," a chapter that might just as appropriately be entitled "Defeat of Paul." After he makes his commit-

ment to his mother not to marry while she lives, the degeneration of his relationship with Miriam accelerates. Although the narrator begins by rendering Paul's narcissistic reactions, he finally turns to Miriam's confused response to Paul's announcement that he cannot love her physically: "[Paul] hated her bitterly at that moment because he made her suffer. Love her! She knew he loved her. He really belonged to her. This about not loving her, physically, bodily was a mere perversity on his part, because she knew she loved him. He was stupid like a child. He belonged to her. His soul wanted her. . . . She guessed somebody had been influencing him. She felt upon him the hardness, the foreignness of another influence." Although the narrator starts by attributing to Miriam both an attitude of condescension and a sense of ownership, this distorted view gives way to a more sympathetic understanding of Miriam's plight. The preceding and subsequent events make clear that (1) Paul's "hatred" derives not from making her suffer, but from his obligations to "another influence," Mrs. Morel; (2) his arrested sexual development does make him behave rather "like a child."

Lawrence's use of omniscience to render a spurious version of Miriam's thinking is an example of what we might call the aesthetics of distortion. A significant breakdown in narrative distance occurs when the narrator accepts Paul's interpretation of Miriam's response to his terminating of their relationship ("The Test on Miriam"). She protests that Paul has always been fighting to free himself. Neither Paul nor the narrator realizes that her response is defensive, deriving from her "self-mistrust." Seeking a reason to make her the scapegoat, Paul becomes enraged that "she had hidden all her condemnation from him, had flattered him, and despised him." Intellectually, the narrator knows that Paul's indignation is inappropriate and hyperbolic, but he cannot bring himself to condemn Paul. In consecutive paragraphs, he renders Paul's consciousness with gentle irony and Miriam's with bitter, scathing irony. Paul's adolescent and exaggerated response is presented in a series of short, almost choppy, declarative sentences to parody logical thought; the quality of his clichéd thinking is self-indicting. Yet, despite his guise of critically observing Paul, the narrator's presentation of her thoughts seems to confirm Paul's belief that he is the wronged party in the relationship:

> He sat in silence. He was full of a feeling that she had deceived him. She had despised him when he thought she

worshipped him. She had let him say wrong things, and had not contradicted him. She had let him fight alone. But it stuck in his throat that she had despised him whilst he thought she worshipped him. . . . All these years she had treated him as if he were a hero, and thought of him secretly as an infant, a foolish child. Then why had she left the foolish child to his folly? His heart was hard against her.

But both this passage and the one that immediately follows are inconsistent with the Miriam whom we know. Can we believe that her mind has worked in Machiavellian ways to entrap subtly a man whom she regards as a "foolish child" and as a "baby":

Why this bondage for her? . . . Why was she fastened to him? . . . She would obey him in his trifling commands. But once he was obeyed, then she had him in her power, she knew, to lead him where she would. She was sure of herself. Only, this new influence! Ah, he was not a man! He was a baby that cries for the newest toy. And all the attachment of his soul would not keep him. Very well, he would have to go. But he would come back when he had tired of his new sensation.

According to the narrator, Miriam deliberately manipulates her "bondage" into "conquest" by seeming to obey while actually taking the lead. After experimenting with other relationships, Paul will return to her because he is a captive of her will, an instrument to fulfill her narcissistic needs, and a child who needs a tolerant mother figure. (Such a view of Miriam gives validity to the indignation that the narrator shares with Paul.)

The reader knows that Miriam does not think in these terms and realizes that the narrator is attributing these motives to her as a means of extenuating Paul, who has been increasingly exploiting her. Her love for nature, her idealism, and her spiritual quest to make it clear that even if she were to lack vitality and passion (as Paul and the narrator incorrectly assume), she surely is not lacking in integrity and dignity. The Miriam of the novel may temporarily oversimplify her relationship to Paul as a "battle" from the beginning, but she is not a Machiavellian of sexual politics capable of loving the man she *despises*. If she is bitter, sufficient reasons are found in the narrative.

Paul cannot commit himself to her, while she can to him. Despite her self-mistrust and masochism, her bondage is the pathetic one of the woman who loves not wisely but too well. The above passages also inadvertently reveal how the Jessie-Miriam relationship in its nonsexuality helped compensate for the childhood of which Lawrence had been partially deprived by his mother's demands. That Miriam, the narrator, and even Paul use the child metaphor for Paul indicates that Lawrence suspected that his oedipal relationship had arrested his sexual *and* emotional development.

The narrator's insistence that Paul's infatuation with his mother is a representative rather than an idiosyncratic one, and that it typifies the tragedy of thousands of young men in England, derives from Lawrence's need to believe this. But the novel presents little evidence that others share Paul's particular problems. Morel, Baxter, and Arthur may have various forms of emotional difficulties, but they seem to function sexually. William's problem is not that he is diffident and shy, but that he becomes entrapped by a naive pursuit of what he has been taught by his mother to consider the Better Life. No, the polemic derives from Lawrence's need to generalize his surrogate's sexual difficulties with Miriam.

In the crucial opening paragraph of "The Test on Miriam," Paul wills to try to "get things right" sexually and marry Miriam. (At this point, the intellectual, logical, and almost mechanical process by which he arrives at a decision mimics his mother's process of intellection.) Again we see that the test on Miriam is really the test of Paul's ability to break loose of his mother. In *Fantasia of the Unconscious* (1922) Lawrence might be addressing Paul's problem when he writes:

> Every frenzied individual is told to find fulfillment in love.
> So he tries. Whereas, there is no fulfillment in love. Half
> of our fulfillment comes *through* love, through strong, sen-
> sual love. But the central fulfillment, for a man, is that he
> possess his own soul in strength within him, deep and
> alone. The deep, rich aloneness, reached and perfected
> through love and the passing beyond any further *quest* of
> love.

Paul cannot find joy and fulfillment in an adult relationship because he is possessed *by his mother.* The obtrusive ironic images—the four dead birds, the remains of the cherries on which they had fed (the ripened cherries had at first seemed proleptic of the young couple's sexual maturity)—show how the retrospective narrator takes a morbid view of the sexual consummation and regards it as merely another mutual act of desperation to blur Paul's and Miriam's fundamental incompatibility. Although he uses these fictive devices to suggest that Paul is the *victim* of Miriam's frigidity, the narrator acknowledges that Paul found the coition reasonably satisfying: "He felt as if nothing mattered, as if his living were smeared away into the beyond, near and quite lovable. This strange, gentle reaching-out to death was new to him." If he achieves inner peace in the sexual act, surely Miriam is partly responsible. Intercourse divests him of the values his mother has rooted in him, neutralizes temporarily the urgency and intensity that she has given his life and career, and enables him to experience nature's rhythms and energy. Saying that he feels "so strange and still," he explains to Miriam: "To be rid of our individuality, which is our will, which is our effort—to live effort-less, a kind of curious sleep—that is very beautiful, I think; that is our after-life—our immortality." Moreover, he discovers the stillness and inaction of death and the unknown, aspects of existence that Mrs. Morel has increasingly denied, but that his father instinctively knows. That his mother refuses to accept death reveals her funda-mental incompatibility with nature. She had tried to reincarnate Wil-liam by shifting her love to Paul. Later, she willfully refuses to accept the natural cycle of life after she almost perversely lingers on when illness has reduced her body to a virtual skeleton. Because of his joyous sexual release, Paul does escape from his mother for a mo-ment. His desire to eschew effort and will derives from the pressure of Mrs. Morel's compelling demands upon him. Temporarily, the sex act nullifies his mother's hold on him and makes her values irrel-evant. But precisely because of this, he cannot admit that the sexual relationship is satisfactory. Technical omniscience gives Lawrence the sanction to plead his case. Considering what Paul seems to have achieved, the narrator's criticism of Miriam's giving herself as a "sac-rifice in which she felt something of horror" should be taken as an example of Lawrence's need to believe that Miriam is incapable of passion. In view of her prolonged virginity, her prior repression and self-denigration, we should hardly be surprised if she experiences a moment of awkwardness and self-doubt.

Their sexual consummation is the prelude to the demise of their personal relationship, and Lawrence's speaker must shift the onus to

Miriam. Can one really trust his version of their meeting at Miriam's grandmother's house? Paul's perspective is a subjective one that reflects his own problems, and his interpretation of her looks is moot: "Her hands lifted in a little pleading movement, and he looked at her face, and stopped. Her big brown eyes were watching him, still and resigned and loving; she lay as if she had given herself up to *sacrifice;* there was her body for him; but the look at the back of her eyes, like a creature awaiting *immolation,* arrested him, and all his blood fell back" (my italics). That years of sexual restraint have marked their relationship is reflected by her slight sign of physical reluctance, but this does not necessarily indicate Miriam's disinclination for sex. Although Miriam says that she wants him, the narrator insists that she regards her sexual participation as "sacrificial." Since the religious terminology is within Paul's mind (he has just said to her: "Your face is bright . . . like a transfiguration"), perhaps the terms "sacrifice" and "immolation" should be ascribed to *his* imagination. Paul's need to criticize her at this point is intensified by his having just compared her with his mother: "He thought she gave a feeling of home almost like his mother." The domestic arrangements within the cottage create a situation in which Miriam displaces his mother as the one responsible for caring for him.

Sex as a ritual between master and victim answers both their impulses. If her understanding of her sexual role involves sacrifice and submission, Paul does not discourage her from this. Paul associates sex with death, because he feels guilty for betraying his mother: "As he rode home he felt that he was finally initiated. He was a youth no longer. But why had he the dull pain in his soul? Why did the thought of death, the after-life, seem so sweet and consoling?" That Paul thinks of the word "initiation" in association with "pain" and "death" is revealing because it shows that Paul regards sex as a ritual to be passed through at a cost to oneself—indeed, as a sacrifice. If Paul and Miriam do not achieve a mutual orgasm, is it not in part because his subconscious will not allow him to replace his mother as his primary passion? Since a fulfilling sexual relationship would give a benediction to his friendship with Miriam, Paul has to find fault with it. The narrator tries to muster evidence to support the view that the alleged sexual failure is Miriam's responsibility when he has her cite the lesson she has learned from her mother: "There is one thing in marriage that is always dreadful, but you have to bear it." But Miriam disavows this rubric and is ready to respond to Paul's tenderness and understanding if Paul can manifest these qualities. The reader knows that Paul must severely criticize Miriam now that he has been sleeping with her, because he already belongs to his mother.

IV

No sooner does he begin his sexual relationship with Miriam than his subconscious requires that he discard her and turn his thoughts to Clara. The narrator is not ironic about Paul's rapid reversal of field: "But insidiously, without knowing it, the warmth he felt for Clara drew him away from Miriam, for whom he felt responsible, and to whom he felt he belonged." As he turns from Miriam to Clara, his anxiety and tension ease. Interestingly, when Paul announces that he is breaking off with Miriam, the narrator stresses natural and vital aspects of her appearance that Paul has been ignoring: "She has made herself look so beautiful and fresh for him. She seemed to blossom for him alone." Just as the narrator is very occasionally grudgingly fair to Morel in part 1, so in part 2 he will reluctantly give Miriam her due. But the parallel is instructive precisely because he purports to value Miriam, while he is obviously hostile to Paul's father.

Martz argues that narrative objectivity is resumed in chapter 12 and speaks of Paul's "remarkable self-understanding" in chapter 13. But neither Paul nor the retrospective narrator understands (1) why Paul is attracted to Clara, and then needs to reject her and to reconcile her to Dawes; (2) why he is tempted to revive his relationship with Miriam; and (3) why he is unable to posit a direction for himself after his mother's death. Martz oversimplifies the effect on Paul of his affair with Clara. If it really has a "clarifying, purgatorial" effect, why is Paul as self-conscious, self-doubting, and fretful as he has always been? Although Clara has helped him to discover that sex can be vital and healthy, has it really enabled "them to find a truth" beyond sex? His behavior with Clara is hardly more logical than it is with Miriam. Paul's interpretation of Clara's attitudes and motives is not substantiated by her behavior and conversations, and his criticism of her after their sexual relationship develops derives from his psychic need to separate himself from her, a need that is intensified by his mother's failing health. In chapters 12 through 15, as in chapters 7 through 11, and to a lesser extent in the first six chapters the narrator engages in mythmaking, extenuation of *his* protagonist, and hypothetical theories of conduct that seem inadequate to the phenomena that he presents.

Paul does find limited sexual fulfillment with Clara. In a setting that looks backward to prehistorical time before man inhabited the earth ("The cliff of red earth sloped swiftly down, through trees and bushes, to the river that glimmered and was dark between the foliage") he has sex without real involvement. As the sexual relationship continues and as an emotional tie begins to evolve, he feels that Clara, too, wishes to possess him. Once Mrs. Morel understands that Clara is not a real threat ("It would be hard for any woman to keep him. Her heart glowed; then she was sorry for Clara") she is soon "at her ease." Yet the Puritanical Coppard value system has been inculcated in Paul and he recognizes Clara as a lesser woman than Miriam "if it came to goodness." When the narrator renders Clara's alleged sense of guilt ("After all, she was a married woman, and she had no right even to what he gave her"), we cannot help feeling that he is really revealing his and Paul's discomfort for sleeping with a somewhat older woman who is married to a man not dissimilar to Morel. When Paul arouses Clara as his father had his mother and displaces Baxter, a man who resembles his father in age, manner, and behavior, he slips into the dialect of his father. Paul ritualistically restores Clara to her proper mate as if to compensate for his disloyalty to his father. The very title of the chapter most concerned with Paul and Clara's sexual relationship, "Baxter Dawes," may be indicative of Lawrence's unconscious need to palliate his father's memory even as he tells the tale.

How revealing is the narrator's conception of the ideal sexual relationship; for that ideal involves the very self-sacrifice on the part of the woman that he had condemned in Miriam: "[Clara] took him simply because his need was bigger either than her or him, and her soul was still within her. She did this for him in his need, even if he left her, for she loved him." Because of his noninvolvement with Clara's soul, because he regards her as a sexual object, he can remain comfortably separate from her once the sex act is complete. The narrator accepts Paul's distinctions between sex with Clara and with Miriam, even though the differences are not nearly as clear as they both make them. The sexual act is an "initiation" and "satisfaction" for each, because it transports them from their conscious selves into a timeless world where the processes of the intellect are suspended:

"To know their own nothingness, to know the tremendous living flood which carried them always, gave them rest within themselves. . . . There was a verification which they had had together. Nothing could nullify it, nothing could take it away: It was almost their belief in life." But is this so different from Paul's original response to sex with Miriam? He becomes dissatisfied with Clara because she, too, cannot fulfill his need for impersonal sex (Does he not really mean anonymous sex?). And she is much less satisfactory than Miriam at directing his passive energies—something that his mother has taught him both to expect and require from his women. According to the narrator's argument, Clara needs to arrest the sexual moment because she herself is incomplete. While Paul needs to keep his sexual life "impersonal," she wants to "hold him" and possess him. Yet, paradoxically, he also wants someone to "keep his soul steady." Neither Paul nor the narrator realizes that it is Miriam who would have come closer to Paul's emotional and sexual needs if Paul had been tender and responsive to her.

Paul, however, is uncomfortable *because* of the success of the sex with Clara: "She made him feel imprisoned when she was there, as if he could not get a free deep breath, as if there were something on top of him." Paul cannot accept sexual satisfaction, and needs to discover the ways in which Clara is not quite as sufficient as their joyous coition might indicate: "The baptism of fire . . . was not Clara. It was something that happened because of her, but it was not her." If by "baptism of fire" is meant the capacity to bring about sexual ecstasy and passionate fulfillment, how could any person be any more than a coequal partner? Does not Paul's expectation that Clara should be the autonomous means by which he achieves fulfillment show simultaneously how he places impossible demands upon his partners and how he sees himself as a rather passive participant to whom things are supposed to happen? Clara offers him passion, but he now must define her according to the very standards by which he had once found Miriam appealing but which he had rejected when he discredited her. Rather suddenly, the quest for the Good and Beautiful, the quest that was the catalyst for the evolution of the nonsexual relationship with Miriam, again becomes important. "Here's the seacoast morning, big and permanent and beautiful; there is she, fretting, always unsatisfied, and temporary as a bubble of foam. What does [Clara] mean to me, after all? She represents something, like a bubble of foam, represents the sea. But what is *she*. It's not her

I care for." Apparently, Clara is as wanting in soul and substance as Miriam had been in passion. His fear that Clara will "absorb" him hardly seems appropriate since his kisses seem "detached, hard, and elemental" and since Clara's "mission" is described by the narrator as "separate" from his.

According to the narrator's myth, the passionate relationship with Clara enables Paul to grow and mature because his soul has been fertilized. But what about Clara? The narrator, Paul's surrogate, convinces himself that Paul has been the agent of Clara's revitalization: "It was almost as if she had gained *herself* and stood now distinct and complete. She had received her confirmation. . . . She *knew* now, she was sure of herself. And the same could almost be said of him." Once Clara realizes that she cannot meet his impossible expectations and that Paul will not accept her as she is, she wants to sacrifice herself to her former husband: "She wanted to humble herself to him, to kneel before him. She wanted now to be self-sacrificial." If Paul's psychic games and subsequent rejection cause the experienced and considerably more self-sufficient Clara to lose her sexual pride (for, no matter what the narrator says, "sacrifice" implies not only self-abnegation but submission), it is not surprising that the inexperienced adolescent Miriam had temporarily lost her sexual identity and had begun to worship perversely the young man who could not make love to her.

V

Paul and the narrator envision a linear pattern that dramatizes the development of Paul's consciousness, but the novel itself weaves an enclosing pattern that qualifies, if it does not parody, the final affirmation. The triumph of the mother *within the novel* is such that even Paul's turning away from death and acceptance of himself as a spark in the void are really an acceptance of his mother's notion that one can shape one's life by the sheer force of one's will: "But no, he would not give in. Turning sharply, he walked towards the city's gold phosphorescence. His fists were shut, his mouth set fast. He would not take that direction, to the darkness, to follow her. He walked towards the faintly humming, glowing town, quickly." As he walked toward the city where his mother had dreamed of Paul's economic and social triumph, his expression (shut fists, mouth fast) mirrors hers as she had approached death: "Her mouth gradually shut hard in a line. She was holding herself rigid. . . . He never forgot that hard, utterly lonely and stubborn clenching of her mouth, which persisted for weeks." Grotesquely, Mrs. Morel's will continues to dominate him after her death. In turning from darkness, he turns to another kind of darkness because he has not yet exorcised the ghost of his destructive oedipal relationship. Thus the "drift towards death," the description Lawrence used to describe Paul's plight in the famous letter to Garnett, is an apt description of Paul's final state within the novel. The reader perceives that the narrator who renders the final scene as an affirmation is not yet free of the autobiographical sources. While Paul can withdraw from the Clara-Baxter-Paul triangle, he can never withdraw from the enclosing circle of his mother's influence. "Sometimes he hated [Mrs. Morel] and pulled at her bondage. His life wanted to free itself of her. It was like a circle where life turned back on itself, and got no farther. She bore him, loved him, and his love turned back into her, so that he could not be free to go forward with his own life, really love another woman." That Paul perceives Mrs. Morel in strikingly sexual terms, after her death removes the incest taboo, shows her continuing hold on him: "She lay like a maiden asleep. . . . She lay like a girl asleep and dreaming of her love. . . . He bent and kissed her passionately. But there was coldness against his mouth." When Paul whimpers "mother" at the end of the novel, he completes the formal circle; he has finally and conclusively responded to Mrs. Morel's desperate cry with which part 1 ended: "Oh, my son—my son!"

Sons and Lovers mimes Lawrence's psyche rather than his intent. The unsuccessful struggle of the omniscient narrator to achieve objectivity is as much an agon as the tale of Paul's abortive quest for psychosexual maturity. Reading *Sons and Lovers,* one also experiences the author's creative problems. That the retrospective narrator is hardly more perceptive than the protagonist, that the narrator is an insistent, urgent, and empathetic apologist for Paul, reveals the hold Lawrence's mother had upon his psyche. *Sons and Lovers* stares down the convention that technical distance and authorial omniscience imply objectivity or truth. It invites us to consider how obsessions and psychic needs penetrate a work of art, and transform and distort the intended form into something more complex, more disturbing, and more compelling.

Eros and Metaphor in *Sons and Lovers*

Mark Kinkead-Weekes

> *Sex is the balance of male and female in the universe, the attraction, the*
> *repulsion, the transit of neutrality, the new attraction, the new repulsion,*
> *always different, always new.*
>
> A Propos of Lady Chatterley's Lover

"Intimacy took place"—the old divorce-court formula ludicrously
exposes a problem that can arise whenever anyone tries to talk about
sexual relationship. For of course "intimacy" cannot "take place."
Sexual intercourse and orgasm can take place in such-and-such a
room at five minutes past the hour; but intimacy implies relationship, and relationship grows, extends, develops, changes, through
space and time. A phrase like "sexual relationship" equally conceals
a tension between two very different modes of being. To accentuate
"sexual" is to emphasize the experience of the body that is an experience within the whole private being, the most "intimate" experience in that sense. The central concern is with an act, with a climax
within that act, with a moment of interior being within that climax.
If we accent "relationship," the emphasis moves in the opposite direction: extensive rather than intensive, concerned with continuity
rather than climax, and with complex processes in space and time
rather than a moment, so that the private being is involved in "intimacy" with another, with others, with the world. Yet these are only
emphases, for most of us would recognize something extreme either
in a sexual act that totally excluded any degree of relationship, or in
a relationship which wholly excluded any consideration of sex.

From *Lawrence and Women,* edited by Anne Smith. © 1978 by Vision Press Ltd.

Lawrence's treatment of "sexual relationship" seems, however, intent on maximizing the tension between the opposite emphases. For the degree of interest by police and magistrates in *The Rainbow*, the paintings, and *Lady Chatterley's Lover* bear witness, if witness were needed, to his insistence on direct and detailed representation of sexual feeling and action. He is unmistakably an erotic writer even where there is no possible offence to social conventions. Yet the characteristic language of that representation also insists that sex is a way of talking about something else, so that Eros becomes Metaphor. Sexual activity and consciousness become the vehicle for exploring wider and wider relationships, within people, between them, throughout society, and the connection of man to the universe.

This tension has consequences for the method of discussion, if one is to establish the peculiar vitality of the fiction that so polarizes itself between the intensive moment and the extensive process. One will have to choose particular passages, because only in detail will the qualities of the language, both the erotic and its metaphorical extensiveness, reveal their nature. Yet because Lawrence is so uniquely exploratory a writer, concerned with the development, flux, and change of relationship, one can only see him truly by seeing his art as a continual process of discovery, not only within each novel, but from novel to novel. One cannot generalize about "Lawrence's treatment of sexual relationship" at any stage, without both superficiality and distortion. One has to try to account intensively for moments, and simultaneously for the fact that they are momentary, partial arrestings of a flowing exploration, always moving beyond. . . .

II

I choose from *Sons and Lovers* the scene in which it becomes clear to Paul, as he reacts to the beauty of the night and the scent of flowers in his garden that he will break off his sexual relationship with Miriam.

The language works directly through sense-perception to register, first, a rich beauty and vitality. Moon and sky glow gold and purple; "the air all round seemed to stir with scent, as if it were alive." The "keen perfume" of the pinks "came sharply across the rocking, heavy scent of the lilies." But already within the first response a second has been released: a hint of something threatening, excessive. The scent of madonna lilies comes "stealthily . . . almost as if it were prowling abroad." They seem to exhaust themselves; they "flagged all loose, as if they were panting." The combined perfumes become over-rich, intoxicating; the moon grows flushed, soon it will melt down.

Cutting across the heavy seductiveness however comes a different kind of vitality: the harsh cry of the corncrake, and "like a shock . . . another perfume, something raw and coarse." The language registers now, as against the flushed moon, the darkness; as against the expended lilies leaning, the irises stiff and fleshy; as against the intoxicating perfumes, something brutal. The rhythm of sense-perception reverses the previous process. Now it begins from shock and potential repulsion, but ends by finding "at any rate, . . . something," which precipitates an inner and unthinking decision against one mode of sexuality, one relationship, and for another. The scene is erotic because the flowers are used to project and explore the sexual conflict, the different complexities of attraction and repulsion, that exist unconsciously in Paul but can be made articulate for the reader. Here the natural world becomes a metaphorical vehicle for the flow and recoil of sexual feelings.

The location of the vision is within the character. The associations are Paul's; the language cannot be made emblematic (so that different flowers would adequately "stand for" Miriam and Clara to *us*) without damaging the novel's complexity. The vocabulary is Lawrence's projection of Paul at this moment, and, as it happens, tells us nothing about the author's attitude.

Yet if we replace the scene within the continuum of exploration in the novel, reminding ourselves of other scenes which it reorchestrates or anticipates, we see that we cannot generalize. In the opening chapter, after one of the terrible battles between Paul's parents, Mrs Morel is thrust out of doors into a garden rendered no less powerfully in terms of moonlight, flowers and perfumes. The effect however is quite different, not only because the purpose this time is to reveal at a deeper level what it is and means to be Mrs Morel, but also because the juxtaposition of character and nature involves a critical placing of this character against a dimension she has ignored. And in the scenes with Miriam that anticipate Paul's rejection, there are many kinds of tension between presentation and analysis. If one instanced the communion over the wild rose bush, the vision of the orange moon over the sandhills, and Paul's cruel attack on Miriam as she fondles the daffodil, one would find several modes of interplay between our response to what we see and feel for ourselves, the attitudes of the characters to one another, and what we are told by the narrator. Paul's criticisms become increasingly fierce, culminating in the cruel charge that Miriam's "abnormal craving is to be loved. You aren't positive, you're negative. You absorb, absorb, as if you must fill yourself up with love, because you've got a shortage somewhere." But we cannot take Paul's response as simply valid—though some critics have done so. The dramatic presentation of Miriam creates her in depth and complexity, so that we often become aware that what we know of Miriam ourselves is being simplified or distorted in Paul's rationalizations of his own recoil. We have to allow for the pressure on him, towards that recoil, of the possessive love and jealousy of Mrs Morel, whose judgements he often echoes, but whose taking of him as son-and-lover is demonstrably a crippling "mischief"—though in other ways it is also a vitalizing force. We have to allow for the validity of Miriam's criticisms of Paul—"She wondered why he always claimed to be normal when he was disagreeable." And we are affected in various ways by the flux and reflux of the narrator's sympathies. Sometimes he is involved or even identified with Paul, seeing as he does, blind with his blindnesses. Sometimes he is detached and critical, aware of how Paul's relationship with his mother has made him both victim and victimizer. The fictive life consists in complex interplay between presentation (both dramatic and symbolic), allowing us to see and feel for ourselves, and a *struggle* to analyse in which both the narrator and ourselves have to be involved—involved with Paul's deficiencies, among other things, in order to become capable of understanding and sympathy without simplification. But "D. H. Lawrence," because he is dramatist, symbolist and narrative ironist, as well as commentator, must never be reduced to the narrator's commentary.

If we look back now at the scene from which we started, we can perhaps detect something questionable about the dialectic of Paul's sexual conflict and its momentary resolution, something crude and overheated in its terms—without automatically referring this to Lawrence himself. For the scene is part of a continuum which points forward as well as back. When Paul tells his mother that he will break off with Miriam, closes his teeth unthinkingly on the flower in his mouth, and spits the petals into the fire, there are anticipations of the scattered petals on Clara's breast by the river, and of the "baptism of fire" in erotic scenes like the one in the field where the peewits cry. Yet Paul's relationship with Clara will bring out the crudity of his sexual recoil from the over-heavy sweetness he associates with Miriam, as well as the meaningfulness of his intuition of a selfhood in the irises. With Clara, in "the immensity of passion," the key discoveries turn out to have little to do with the coarse or brutal, and everything to do with a vocabulary of inclusiveness, and stillness-in-the-self. Paul becomes aware of a "strong, strange, wild life, that breathed with his in the darkness through this hour. It was all so much bigger than themselves. . . . They had met, and included in their meeting the thrust of the manifold grass-stems, the cry of the peewit, the wheel of the stars. . . . There was a verification which they had had together. Nothing could nullify it, nothing could take it away; it was almost their belief in life." Or again, "It was as if he, and the stars, and the dark herbage, and Clara were licked up in an immense tongue of flame, which tore onwards and upwards . . . everything was still, perfect in itself, along with him. This wonderful stillness in each thing in itself, while it was being borne along in a very ecstasy of living, seemed the highest point of bliss." The erotic experience becomes a language of organic relation with the natural universe, and of new selfhood.

Yet the exploration continues, and a tentativeness—"almost," "seemed"—still accompanies the apparently big claims. For the relationship of passion, though it brings the lovers into a kind of harmony with the world of nature, does not include enough or create sufficient selfhood. In its impersonality, its immensity, the human being seems devalued. Clara becomes "only a woman," depersonalized; "She represents something, like a bubble of foam represents the sea. But what is *she?* It's not her I care for," "I feel," Clara says, "as if all you weren't there, and as if it weren't *me* you were taking." Because it proves incapable of including the full personality, and the world of conscious awareness in which Paul lives with his mother and lived with Miriam, the erotic relationship itself dwindles and becomes deathly. Paul's tragedy is that while his mother lives, he cannot offer or receive a love which includes the whole of himself; and when she dies, he has only a stubborn refusal to give in, to hold him back from the drift towards death.

I have been trying to bring out the sheer difficulty of completing a sentence that begins "Lawrence's treatment of sexual relationship in *Sons and Lovers*." One cannot extrapolate scenes, because the language at any particular point is partial and temporary, giving up its significance only when it is replaced in a continuum of exploration. One cannot extrapolate authorial attitudes, because generalizations suggest a relation between author and fiction that is false to Lawrence's art. To the purist eye, the fictional process of *Sons and Lovers* is a curious blend of types, both the apparently "omniscient" analysis of complex characters and actions, and the rendering of different consciousnesses by a neutral author. But why is this? I think one glimpses an answer in the language of inclusiveness and self-definition. The certainties of omniscience may not be inclusive enough, and the uncertainties of neutrality may fail to achieve sufficient selfhood in the writer. So Lawrence's method is both a self-projection into different consciousnesses, allowed to produce themselves and expand in their own ways, in order that the vision we get at the end should be inclusive and complicated enough; *and* an insistence on involving himself and his reader in a constant struggle to understand, and relate, and produce an analysis of what a sufficient self should be—particularly since he is writing about his own life. And once we grasp the form, I think we also begin to write our sentence about the theme of sexual relationship. For here too the demand is that there should be two opposite but equally vital processes. On the one hand sex is seen as a mode of inclusiveness, seeking to relate the whole self to the whole other, and both to the rhythms of the natural universe. On the other hand, and at the same time, sex is an opposite process, not only joining-up, but singling out into "each thing in itself." The vocabulary is both a way of using nature to talk about sex, and a way of seeing through the erotic into a relation between men and women, and the universe they inhabit. We see the centrality of sex to Lawrence in the relation of form and theme. The subject is sexual relationship, explored as necessarily inclusive *and* distinctive, searching for the shape of wholeness in the story of failure. The art is both a reaching out from the authorial self into others and the natural world, tentative, exploratory; and an "agonized" analysis in which the author struggles to clarify himself.

The scene we began from finally reveals its basic dialectic in the same opposition, in rhythms of complex attraction and repulsion: the lilies leaning, calling; the irises stiff, upright in themselves.

Reading *Sons and Lovers*

E. P. Shrubb

It is a truism that our sense of the "life" in a work of art seems often
to have to do with our sense not only that what the work of art
achieves is not the record of a triumph, say, but the exploration of a
conflict, but also, and further, that the opposing forces or powers in
it are being held not just in balance but in changing balance. It is no
less true, but perhaps less a truism, that a special vividness can
quicken this sense of "life" as we come to believe that in the work of
art we have an account or record of conflict given not only *by* the
artist but also, so to speak, *through* him; if nowadays we can no
longer think comfortably in terms of daemons and Muses, we may
nevertheless feel the need of metaphor to express our sense that a
work of art, just as a child is the product of its parents but something
new too, may be the creature of its artist but have not only a separate
but an independent—*un*created, almost—nature and being.

Some such notions may come to the mind of a critical reader
setting out on the opening paragraph of *Sons and Lovers*.

> "The Bottoms" succeeded to "Hell Row." Hell Row was a
> block of thatched, bulging cottages that stood by the
> brook-side on Greenhill Lane. There lived the colliers who
> worked in the little gin-pits two fields away. The brook
> ran under the alder-trees, scarcely soiled by these small
> mines, whose coal was drawn to the surface by donkeys

From *Sydney Studies in English* 6 (1980–81). © 1981 by E. P. Shrubb.

that plodded wearily in a circle round a gin. And all over the countryside were these same pits, some of which had been worked in the time of Charles II, the few colliers and the donkeys burrowing down like ants into the earth, making queer mounds and little black places among the corn-fields and the meadows. And the cottages of these coalminers, in blocks and pairs here and there, together with odd farms and homes of the stockingers, straying over the parish, formed the village of Bestwood.

With a name like "The Bottoms," you can't be quite thought to have won a victory over, even if you have succeeded to, "Hell Row." If things have improved, there is room for more improvement still, the balance is not settled. And if we take as a sign of life the wry jocundity with which the two names are displayed, in all their bare vulgarity (though "bottom" here refers, of course, to low-lying land, not to the human posterior), then the impression is not contradicted by the account we are given in the next sentence of Hell Row, an account that makes its name seem quite inappropriate; what is hellish about "thatched" (not hard black slate, at least), "bulging" (not skinny and thin, at least, and perhaps even plump?), "cottages" (not shacks or cabins or huts, at least) standing "by the brook-side" (which is at least a natural stream of water) on (the quite Wordsworthian) "Greenhill Lane" is not immediately evident. And if we learn a little later that Hell Row was "notorious," that it had "acquired an evil reputation," then all we learn by way of justification of that reputation is that it was acquired "through growing old," which seems less of a sin as each day passes, but of course is not quite what you'd choose in a plumbing system or (which is probably more relevant to any consideration of Hell Row) a roof in the rain or a wall in the wind.

The only justification for spending any time thinking about Hell Row at all—apart from the interest that always attaches to the point where hammer and chisel cut that first chip out of the marble block, and apart from the little local puzzle of its name—is that homes are important in *Sons and Lovers.* One would not wish to retitle it *House and Garden,* quite, but it is in a deep way no accident that the first sentence of the novel is about an improvement in accommodation; the emphasis throughout the novel on the kitchens that life takes place in is something no reader could fail to notice, and each move to a new house is prominently recorded. It is no accident that the first passage of detailed description in the novel is of the Bottoms, and it is no accident that the first sentence we read about the first Morel mentioned is this:

> Mrs Morel was not anxious to move into the Bottoms, which was already twelve years old and on the downward path, when she descended to it from Bestwood.

I keep saying it is "no accident" because these references to homes are beads on a strong thread that runs through the whole novel; I have no way of telling whether or not Lawrence gave such attention to accommodation in these opening pages out of a conscious awareness of everything homes were to "mean" in his novel. Questions about a novelist's intentions are always otiose, if for no other reason than because what any mature adult knows about his own intentions, let alone anyone else's, is that he doesn't know much about them; but part of what I mean by saying these references are "no accident" is perhaps that there does seem to be something *un-*conscious about them, that they do not give the impressions of being the product of an accidental or contingent intention, but rather the product of an interest or concern that Lawrence didn't make the book out of but rather made the book out of Lawrence. And I suppose that to speak of such an "impression" is to respond to my sense that nowhere in these opening pages is there to be detected—in a novel heavily weighted with theories—any theory at all about the Bottoms and Hell Row; nothing in them betrays a "mental" origin.

It's history, indeed, that the opening paragraph seems to be providing us with, an account of what happened, not of what people thought, and not of what people thought had happened. It takes us as far back as to Charles II, thus locating this sort of mining in a decidedly preindustrial past, where miners walk to work not down streets but across fields—as indeed Walter Morel still does—where mines are part not of the town but of the countryside, where they make "queer mounds," perhaps like the ones some insects or animals make, and "little black places," perhaps like the ones men make with fires, "among the corn-fields and the meadows." The miners' homes take their place amongst, not in distinction to, the farms and the homes of the handweaving stockingers. If nostalgic readers might find in this picture some corner of an ideal world, they should nevertheless keep it clear in their minds that *Sons and Lovers* is not offering it as an ideal; it comes to us neutral, as history, free (so far as anything ever is) of value-judgment. The word "queer" makes this as explicit as can be: "queer" here means "I don't quite know what to think (of the mounds)"; and "little black places" comes to us as uninterpreted clues noted from the site of a crime might. Perhaps it's because of this appearance of neutrality—in which the word "parish" is nearly, but not quite, merely a title deed or even geographical term—that the word "formed" so easily does its work of making a whole of what has come before.

The balance created—in the prose as in the history—between brook and pit is of course immediately to be disturbed.

> Then, some sixty years ago, a sudden change took place. The gin-pits were elbowed aside by the large mines of the financiers. The coal and iron field of Nottinghamshire and Derbyshire was discovered. Carston, Waite and Co. appeared. Amid tremendous excitement, Lord Palmerston formally opened the company's first mine at Spinney Park, on the edge of Sherwood Forest.

What do we make of "elbowed?" What do we think of "financiers?" In the first paragraph there is work and difficulty—the donkeys plod wearily, and the men burrow like ants—but there is no elbowing of anything; things stand and live side by side, and the brook is "scarcely soiled" by the pit. There is a rough vigour in the "elbowed"—but it is an ugly rough vigour? Perhaps we simply have to wait and see. Are financiers ugly? Who knows? All the sentence perhaps allows us to think about them is that they are gross, somehow; their mines are "large." Certainly the rest of this second paragraph speaks not of ugliness but of the thrills of discovery and new beginnings. Its excitement too comes to rest, finally, with not an invasion but a contiguity; the first mine is "at Spinney Park" (not in it), and "on the edge of Sherwood Forest" (so Robin Hood's undisturbed).

This impression of coexistence is reinforced by what we read soon about that symbol of industrial Britain, the railway:

> From Nuttall, high up on the sandstone among the woods, the railway ran, past the ruined priory of the Carthusians and past Robin Hood's Well, down to Spinney Park, then on to Minton, a large mine among corn-fields; from Minton across the farm-lands of the valleyside to Bunker's Hill, branching off there, and running north to

Beggarlee and Selby, that looks over at Crich and the hills of Derbyshire; six mines like black studs of the country-side, linked by a loop of fine chain, the railway.

But perhaps that is, as it were, the view from an aeroplane, from which everything looks pretty; reading about the Bottoms, we are presented with the contrast between the prettiness of the fronts and the ugliness of the backs, a contrast there is no apparent hope of making a whole of. The brook and the pit seem to have parted company; industrialism is making, in what was once a whole world, its own world, and that is the world in which men, women and children will now live:

> And between the rows, between the long lines of ash-pits, went the alley, where the children played and the women gossipped and the men smoked. So, the actual conditions of living in the Bottoms, that was so well built and that looked so nice, were quite unsavoury because people must live in the kitchen, and the kitchens opened on to that nasty alley of ash-pits.

Sons and Lovers is quite decidedly about the separations industrialism makes. One could make out a case, I think, that the problems Paul and Miriam have with one another, if they cannot in a simple way be attributed to the consequences of industrialism, have their connections with the educational possibilities the towns that industrialism creates make available to the young Morels—and of course to Miriam—as they were not made available to Walter Morel. In the later parts of the book, indeed, Paul is constantly on the move between brook, as it were, and pit, books under his arm. When Paul becomes a kind of machine-world stockinger, at Jordan's, the pages fill with intimations of disease—Jordan's make, after all, *surgical* appliances—disorder and disaster. Mr Pappleworth's chlorodyne gum contains, one presumes, or is believed by the people who buy it to contain chloroform, morphia, tincture of Indian hemp, prussic acid, and other substances. Fanny is a hunchback. Susan is forced into marriage by an unwanted pregnancy. In the midst of it all, Clara Dawes sits like a great Jersey cow tangled in a wire fence, or the princess locked in a tower because she married the frog; Paul has to take her back to beside the brook, the Trent, away from the pit, to make love to her. (But I suppose that's understandable enough.)

Mr Jordan, the authority figure with no natural authority, and

Baxter Dawes, who has some kind—or is offered as having some kind—of natural authority—it is he, after all, who elbows Mr Jordan not only aside but right through the swing door and down the stairs—but is mostly either drunk or ill, both have their parts to play here, but it is significant of the achievement of the novel that Jordan's is by no means a *demonstration* of disease and disorder and disaster; it is a place where Fanny's beautiful hair reminds us of the natural flow of things, where the girls all sing together, unseparated, and it is in the complexity of the forces at work in the scenes, the shifting balances among them, that we find out experience of Jordan's, not in any simple diagrammatic or algebraic significance derivable or translatable from them. It's hard to believe that these passages of life at Jordan's are the product of Lawrence's analytic thinking—partly, perhaps, because though there is a great deal we can think about them, they do not reduce to thoughts, they cannot be summed up in views or ideas.

If, when we read of Paul looking for job advertisements that he was already a "prisoner of industrialism," it may occur to us that there is someone we have been reading about who is even more a prisoner. Mrs Morel is of course at the center of the novel—her marriage begins it, and her death ends it—and she is the first individual the book singles out for us. And the first thing we learn about her is that she "was not anxious to move into the Bottoms." Mrs Morel has married beneath her, and more and more as the book proceeds finds her husband a disappointment. The first disappointment, appropriately enough, has to do with accommodation—she discovers that the house Walter has allowed her to believe he owns is in fact his mother's—and when we first meet her it is her middle-class concern for isolated security that we are put in touch with, the security of the separateness being in "your own home" gives:

> She had an end house in one of the top blocks, and thus had only one neighbour; on the other side an extra strip of garden. And, having an end house, she enjoyed a kind of aristocracy among the other women of the "between" houses, because her rent was five shillings and sixpence instead of five shillings a week. But this superiority of station was not much consolation to Mrs Morel.

It was not much consolation, of course, not only because she is pregnant, and shrinks a little from her first contact with "the Bottoms women"; it is not much consolation because her husband was a miner.

What exacerbates the divisions industrialism brings about in this society is, in the case of the Morels' private, domestic society, class difference. The chief surface evidence of this, of course, is in the languages members of the family speak. Walter Morel speaks a working-class language, and the rest of the family speak an educated middle-class language; and it is hard, sometimes, not to think of Walter's as the language of feeling and Mrs Morel's as the language of thought. Being the language of thought, it is the language of progress and success in the new world; William's letter, as well as Paul's knowledge of French, get Paul his job at Jordan's. (It is also, of course, the language in which novels are written, and that perhaps is one of the many reasons why Paul did well to cleave so to his mother.) Language opens up the way ahead:

> When the children were old enough to be left, Mrs Morel joined the Women's Guild. It was a little club of women attached to the Co-operative Wholesale Society, which met on Monday night in the long room over the grocery shop of the Bestwood "Co-op." The women were supposed to discuss the benefits to be derived from co-operation, and other social questions. Sometimes Mrs Morel read a paper. It seemed queer to the children to see their mother, who was always busy about the house, sitting writing in her rapid fashion, thinking, referring to books, and writing again. They felt for her on such occasions the deepest respect.

While the novel does not direct us to make the comparison, a reader may very well take the opportunity it offers him to think about the women at Jordan's in connection with Mrs Morel and her Women's Guild. The women who wish to improve things—and incidentally, we may very well ask ourselves if there is not in the sentence "The women were supposed to discuss the benefits to be derived from co-operation, and other social questions" a faint ridiculing smile, suppressed only by the reverence the end of paragraph so good humouredly and generously gives—first of all have to leave their children—which of course it is perfectly understandable that they must do, but which the paragraph makes an opening point of, nevertheless, as a piece of music, which must be in *some* key, nevertheless sets off in a particular key—secondly, must work quite alone, in their heads, instead of being "busy about the house," and thirdly, create a division between themselves and their husbands:

> From off the basis of the Guild, the women could look at their homes, at the conditions of their own lives, and find fault. So the colliers found their women had a new standard of their own, rather disconcerting.

In her home, Mrs Morel seems often to be functioning as a little Women's Guild all of her own.

The girls at Jordan's seem different:

> Below him (Paul) saw a room with windows round two sides, and at the farther end half a dozen girls sitting bending over the benches in the light from the window, sewing. They were singing together "Two Little Girls in Blue." Hearing the door opened, they all turned round, to see Mr. Pappleworth and Paul looking down on them from the far end of the room. They stopped singing.

What the language here emphasizes, quite forcefully, is the cohesiveness of the girls. If the ladies (as one must call them) at the Women's Guild also make a group, then it is a fact about them that the novel never bothers to realize for us; what is dramatized for us of the Women's Guild is not that it is a group, but that it makes for individual separateness. We are told that Women's Guild activities make for sexual division, and the lively confrontations between the Jordan's girls and Mr Pappleworth are dramatized; what they seem to have in common, that is, is merely thought about in connection with the Women's Guild, whereas it is seen in the life in connection with Jordan's.

In the community at Jordan's, however, there is one separate individual, Clara Dawes.

> During the ten years that she had belonged to the women's movement she had acquired a fair amount of education, and, having had some of Miriam's passion to be instructed, had taught herself French, and could read in that language with a struggle. She considered herself as a woman apart, and particularly apart, from her class. The girls in the spiral department were all of good homes. It was a small, special industry, and had a certain distinction.

> There was an air of refinement in both rooms. But Clara
> was aloof also from her fellow workers.

All the elements we have been picking up seem to be represented
here. The women's movement, closely relating to the Guild, is there;
education, and in particular education in a foreign language, is there;
"good homes" and "industry" meet; middle-class "refinement" enters; and we are offered the image of a single, separate, *superior* individual. If we have here the loose net in which Paul and his mother,
and Miriam, and Clara, hang together—we could perhaps even suggest that Miriam and her mother form a small amateur Women's
Guild: they certainly feel quite separate from the Leivers men—then
it has been on his mother's shoulders that Paul has stood to see where
to go.

> "I *do* like to talk to her—I never said I didn't. But I *don't*
> love her."
> "Is there nobody else to talk to?"
> "Not about the things we talk of. There's lots of things
> that you're not interested in, that—"
> "What things?" Mrs Morel was so intense that Paul be-
> gan to pant.
> "Why—painting—and books. *You* don't care about
> Herbert Spencer."
> "No," was the sad reply. "And *you* won't at my age."
> "Well, but I do now—and Miriam does—"
> "And how do you know," Mrs Morel flashed defiantly,
> "that *I* shouldn't. Do you ever try me!"

From the vantage-point his mother established for him, Paul can
peer into the distant lands of French and Herbert Spencer, and Miriam and Clara peer with him.

In its analysis of the process of industrialization, *Sons and Lovers*
has much more to bring before us than even all this, more than Jordan's girls and the Guild and education, more even than French and
Herbert Spencer; it has, for example, the story of William. It is immediately after the paragraphs devoted to the Guild that William's
comet career is set in motion.

> Then, when the lad was thirteen, she got him a job in the
> "Co-op." office. He was a very clever boy, frank, with
> rather rough features and real viking blue eyes.
> "What does want ter ma'e a stool-harsed Jack on 'im

for?" said Morel. "All he'll do is to wear his britches behind out, an' earn nowt. What's 'e startin' wi'?"

"It doesn't matter what he's starting with," said Mrs
Morel.

"It wouldna! Put 'im 'i th' pit wi' me, an e'll earn a easy
ten shillin' a wik from th' start. But six shillin' wearin' his
truck-end out on a stool's better than ten shillin' i' th' pit
wi' me, I know."

"He is *not* going in the pit," said Mrs Morel, "and there's
an end of it."

"It wor good enough for me, but it's non good enough
for 'im."

It's no good asking if William would have been better off "i' th' pit"
with his father—or, for that matter, if Paul would have, or even Miriam—but we can ask what not going down the mine brought him,
and the answer is first Gyp and then death. Even Herbert Spencer is
preferable, and if Paul managed to pull himself out of the "lapse
towards death" only for that, he is even so decidedly better off than
his brother. William, who like his father spent all day and his life's
vigour at the Wakes, took a vigorous fling, as no one else in the novel
does, at the world's goods, at the world in which even a woman is
not much more than a good—a photograph, and scores of pairs of
gloves—and found that what he had to pay for everything was
everything. It's possible, even, that he died because he was alone,
separated off from family and home. In Gyp we have another instance of the sexual attractiveness of the middle class; William has
fallen for the refinement his father fell for before him.

But Walter Morel not only does not go under, not only does not
die; he survives them all—he nearly even survives Paul. Why? the
language in which he criticizes his wife's determination to keep William out of the pit is, surely, part of what saves him. It preserves him
in the world of the working class, saves him, for one thing, from
earning the sort of money in the sorts of conditions that free William
to try for the things that money in the city is invited by it to try for.
His language, also, is a language of men; it is not even the language
his mother speaks, which, like the snippets we hear from other
working-class women in the novel, is not vivid, but only ill-
educated. It is the women who—in *Sons and Lovers,* that is—are the
sources of the desire for improvement, sources of dissatisfaction

with the existing state of affairs; Walter, as his conversation about William's first job makes clear, seeks only continuance, not improvement.

But it is in the minor poetry of his speech, in the self-renewing vigour of it, that we find the evidence of what preserves him from the fate of William, from being made the creature of his wife. Love-talk in as late a novel as *Lady Chatterley's Lover* comes in a dialect like Walter's: that's often what is meant by calling it the language of feeling. But Walter makes it clear that there are more feelings than love; it is not love that he's talking, when he says William should go down the pit. Or is it? Love is certainly a good deal of what this novel, like most others, is about, and continuance is made possible, I suppose one must concede, by love. But we don't need quite such profundities to think with, looking at the speech of Walter Morel. The earthy, elbowing vigour of "stool-harsed" should make most of us stool-harsed Jacks writhe a little, at the spondaic punch in it first, and then at what force has done, which is to imagine us as having wooden bottoms, as being not fully human in that distinguished area, Pinocchios without the magic. All such a man wears out, Walter Morel implies, is not muscle but trousers. We hear another spondee hammer in "earn nowt," hear another rhetorical door slam, and perhaps respond to the belief that seems to be behind it, that it is part of a man's life to earn his way, rather than, say, to be paid for serving on a stool. And what goes along with these explosive phrases is the sinuous flow suggested in all the elisions. The vigour is not only blunt, but supple too.

The concreteness of Walter's imagery—the "six shillin'," the "truck-end," the "stool," the "pit"—a continuing mark of his speech. Morel is the maker, and his wife is the thinker; if we think of him, we very likely soon think of Taffy the donkey, or the mouse, of the fuses, or the coal-rake, or the white calico snap-bag, or the drops of fat he caught on his bread as he toasted his bacon on a fork. These are the things of his life, and of his speech. And it's in his life, not just in his talk or his ambitions, that these things coexist. Mrs Morel smells her flowers, and delights in them; Morel

> appeared at the pit-top, often with a stalk from the hedge between his teeth, which he chewed all day to keep his mouth moist, down the mine, feeling quite as happy as when he was in the field.

If the brook and the pit come together anywhere in the novel after the first few paragraphs, then probably it is in the life of Walter Morel that they do it.

There is a distinct danger, in this line of thinking about *Sons and Lovers,* of sentimentalizing or romanticizing Walter. A great deal can be said for the community of men—something like the equivalent of the girls at Jordan's—that Walter and his workmates create, but it finds its second home—after the pit—in the pub, and though we do not know enough about life in the pub—we know little more than Mrs Morel knows, indeed: she thinks about it for us—to be able to come to an informed conclusion about what it amounts to, there is no turning away from the drunkenness that seems ineradicable in it. How much less damaging it might have been to both of them had Walter lurched home to a less Congregationalist welcome than his wife gave him, it is impossible to say, of course; but there is no denying the power of such a passage as this:

> Having such a great space in front of the house gave the children a feeling of night, of vastness, and of terror. This terror came in from the shrieking of the tree and the anguish of the home discord. Often Paul would wake up, after he had been asleep a long time, aware of thuds downstairs. Instantly he was wide awake. Then he heard the booming shouts of his father, come home nearly drunk, then the sharp replies of his mother, then the bang, bang of his father's fist on the table, and the nasty snarling shout as the man's voice got higher. And then the whole was drowned in a piercing medley of shrieks and cries from the great, wind-swept ash-tree. The children lay silent in suspense, waiting for a lull in the wind to hear what their father was doing. He might hit their mother again.

The poetry of such a passage speaks most intensely of the plight of the Morel children. Placing them high up, in the world, as it were, of only time and space, not substance—that is down below, down where the powerful forces of the earth's movers are, one of whom actually comes from underground—high up amongst spirit-noises of the air but passive auditors still of the earthquake rumblings and thuds below, the passage dramatizes vividly the powerless isolation of the children; that psychological damage may follow from the general vague impression they might build up that the passions of adulthood are inseparable from brutality is easy to understand.

The Walter who, through his wife or not, has this effect on his children cannot be sentimentalized out of existence in favour of the Walter who is so nice to Taffy. Part of the analysis of industrialism is to be found in the prominence the novel gives to the destructive consequences of alcoholism. We must remember, of course, as well, that it is not Walter who is destroyed; his drunkenness is not in any way the equivalent of Mrs Morel's cancer. If he is Lawrence's chief drunk, he is not the only hero (shall we say?) of Lawrence's to find that all his life needs cannot be found in a kitchen, and walk out of it, to find that the world of men and work is opposed by, not complemented by, wife and children and kitchen and garden. The men who manage it are the rather dull Leonard, colourless (though also not unmanly) Arthur, and Baxter Dawes. The men who don't are Paul and William and, to the degree that his marriage was not a success, Walter.

The lack of success of that marriage, however, is the success of the novel, many readers feel; the first six chapters—up to the chapter entitled "Lad-and-Girl Love"—are the novel's central achievement. It is after these chapters, of course, that Walter's appearances become much less frequent, and his spirit less evident. Speaking to Miriam on one occasion, Paul says, "I don't believe God knows such a lot about Himself. God doesn't *know* things, He *is* things. And I'm sure He's not soulful," and while it would be taking things rather far to substitute Walter's name there for God's—and of course nothing could be further from Paul's mind just then—it is perhaps in some such terms that one might find a way of summing Walter's importance up; and perhaps one could go further, and suggest that, in a general way, what is less satisfactory about part 2 of the novel is that it is soulful in the constant presence of the adolescent Paul and Miriam, whose fairly constant interest is in (though the distinction is a rough one) knowing as against being.

What Paul is seeking for himself through part 2 is, perhaps, the wholeness of "being" as against the separateness of "knowing." The particular state of wholeness he's after is the state in which the spirit is made flesh, in which love is fulfilled, in which marriage (as holy and bodily made one) is consummated. All he achieves in the long run is the remaking of his parents' marriage in giving Baxter back to Clara—and it's not the other way round—and setting off, himself, for the town, after the death of his mother, to try again.

His difficulty is associated, in a central passage of diagnosis, with his parents'.

> A good many of the nicest men he knew were like himself, bound in by their own virginity, which they could not break out of. They were so sensitive to their women that they would go without them for ever rather than do them a hurt, an injustice. Being the sons of mothers whose husbands had blundered brutally through their feminine sanctities, they were themselves too diffident and shy. They could easier deny themselves than incur any reproach from a woman; for a woman was like their mother, and they were full of the sense of their mother.

Hey up, there! What's this about brutal blundering?

> She looked at him, startled. This was a new tract of life suddenly opened before her. She realized the life of the miners, hundreds of them toiling below earth and coming up at evening. He seemed to her noble. He risked his life daily, and with gaiety. She looked at him, with a touch of appeal in her pure humility.
>
> "Shouldn't ter like it?" he asked tenderly. "'Appen not, it 'ud dirty thee." She had never been "thee'd" and "thou'd" before.
>
> The next Christmas they were married, and for three months she was perfectly happy; for six months she was very happy.

Even Paul seems to know that.

> "Yes; but my mother, I believe, got *real* joy and satisfaction out of my father at first. I believe she had a passion for him; that's why she stayed with him. After all, they were bound to each other."
>
> "Yes," said Miriam.
>
> "That's what one *must have,* I think," he continued— "the real, real flame of feeling through another person— once, only once, if it only lasts three months. See, my mother looks as if she's *had* everything that was necessary for her living and developing. There's not a tiny bit of feeling of sterility about her."

"No," said Miriam.

"And with my father, at first, I'm sure she had the real thing. She knows; she has been there. You can feel it about her, and about him, and about hundreds of people you meet every day; and, once it has happened to you, you can go on with anything and ripen."

"What has happened, exactly?" asked Miriam.

"It's so hard to say, but the something big and intense that changes you when you really come together with somebody else. It almost seems to fertilize your soul and make it that you can go on and mature."

But Mrs Morel puts a scotch in the wheel, rather, when she tells Paul, whose mouth is on her throat (kissing it) and who a few moments later very overheatedly acts Hamlet to his Gertrude by telling her not to sleep with his father:

"And I've never—you know, Paul—I've never had a husband—not really"

although earlier in the same chapter we have read this:

"You should have seen him as a young man," she cried suddenly to Paul, drawing herself up to imitate her husband's once handsome bearing.

Morel watched her shyly. He saw again the passion she had had for him. It blazed upon her for a moment. He was shy, rather scared, and humble. Yet again he felt his old glow. And then immediately he felt the ruin he had made during these years. He wanted to bustle about, to run away from it.

So what's the truth of the matter, if there is one? The first passage emerges from a longish piece of dramatized, reflective self-analysis in which Paul wonders why he is reluctant to be with Miriam, and decides that the obstacle lies in his shrinking from "physical contact." The passage refers to "the nicest men he knew," but are we to conclude from that that these general notions about "virginity" in young men are indeed Paul's notions? Who are these "nicest men?" Not prominent characters in *Sons and Lovers*. Whoever they are, how did whoever knew them—Paul or Lawrence—know that their fathers had "blundered rather brutally" through the "feminine sanctities" of their mothers? It sounds like the *last* thing a "nice" man would tell to even a close friend, and the last thing a mother who'd had "feminine sanctities" would tell a son.

And what are "feminine sanctities?" Little rooms all papered over with chintz doilies? Drawers filled with not legs but lavender? One is entitled to be disrespectful, I suggest, by what is implied in "they were so sensitive to their women that they would go without them for ever rather than do them a hurt, and injustice." "Their women" indeed! (for although "their" is not merely possessive, it has some of the crudeness of possessiveness in it). "Go without them" indeed! (as if "their women" were a tempting chocolate pudding, as if their "feminine sanctities" were all there was to "them"). "Rather than do them a hurt" indeed! (as if this whole way of thinking were not itself a "hurt," and "injustice," as if to "go without them" were not itself a "hurt").

This is a piece of bad writing because it is a piece of bad feeling; it is a piece of bad feeling because it is not alive and alert to its subject, it has not *realized* its subject. That is not to say, of course, that there is not a subject there, waiting to be brought to life; male crudeness and female delicacy are as real as their opposites, and the consequences in the children of a marriage in which male crudeness has invaded female delicacy may very well be disabling. But no lines of life run from this passage to the great sources of the novel's energy of narration. Paul seems to make some sort of a fist of breaking out of virginity, for a start. Mrs Morel does not seem to have been blundered into. Paul incurs enough reproach to be getting on with.

That there are things to be thought about here, issues raised— about boyish and girlish modesty, as well as about the spiritualization of sex—that have to do with *Sons and Lovers* is clear, but I suggest that the bad feeling—and (what goes with that) bad thinking—is one of the signs that a difficulty is being evaded. The very generalness of the language is a hint—in the context of, say, Beatrice and Arthur, Annie and Leonard, William and Gyp, and even Walter and Gertrude—that the real source of Paul's problem has not been found, and perhaps that its discovery is not actually desired.

In the second of those five passages, Walter has just offered to take Gertrude down the mine, and the offer, coming freshly on the heels of her surprise at having met a miner, startles a small vision in her, which the language of the passage quite delicately makes real to us. The awkward phrase "tract of life"—"tract" faintly whispering

"pamphlet" in our ears, and murmuring of the merely geographical—allows us to sense Gertrude's own awkwardness. The faintly
biblical "toiling below earth" helps us to understand that "realized"
has something mental, conceptual, in its "real," and at the end of the
sentence we meet the gentleness of "evening," and perhaps its senti-
mentality, leading as it does to "noble," which *we* have had no evidence that Walter is. But his tenderness rings true; his concern, as his
little speech makes clear, *is* tender. And if we want to know what
sort of happiness she had for three months, the intimacy of being
"thee'd" and "thou'd" gives us our answer; she was tenderly loved,
in a way her father, we guess, could never have made conceivable
to her.

When we come to Paul thinking about all this, what's immediately striking is the wordiness of all he says. If there is some kind of
truth in it all—and our evidence is that there certainly is so far as his
mother and father are concerned (but what a curious coincidence it
is that he says "three months": surely only the novel knew *that*)—
nevertheless one might wonder that Paul does not see his *father* as
being free of "sterility" (though it *is*, of course, Clara that the conversation is thinking about) and that Miriam has so little to offer in
it, is a mere interlocutor (though one could argue that this is because
Paul's thoughts are entering an area Miriam has never ventured into).
One wonders again who are these "hundreds of people you meet
every day," and how far "big and intense" takes us, or the repetitive-
ness that perhaps tries to *will* into being "the real, real flame of feeling;" one might wonder, more generally, about the notion that if
someone seems not "sterile" then it must be because he—or rather,
she—has had three months of "*real* joy and satisfaction," which is
different (presumably) from just joy and satisfaction, in (presumably) sex. Miriam might well ask what has happened.

Paul is young, sex is important, some people are more mature
than others; but the novel is not making much attempt, in passages
like this, to show that it knows more about all that than Paul knows.
It seems stuck where he is stuck, in a *belief* that wholeness of being
has something to do with successful, or satisfactory, or fulfilling,
sex, or sexual love.

About the last pages of chapter 8, where we have Gertrude telling Paul she's never had a husband—and, a little later, have a duel, a
fainting mother, and Paul's request that she abjure the marital bed
(and it's the same mother who, much later, is given a poisonous po-

tion to drink, for what that's worth)—it's as hard to think, I find, as it would be about molten lava you might find yourself looking at through a crack in a garden bed one fine morning. The easy thing is to say something about Oedipus and pass on, or by; but the problem is not to find a label, but to see how the lava connects with the garden; I am tempted to say that lava is so out of character in a garden that it cannot be assimilated to it, that lava does not explain gardens except in the most unhelpful way, the way nuclear reactions in the sun explain Surfers Paradise. Its importance, I suggest, is to alert us to the possibility that there are powers in this novel that hardly find expression—they are not what we see in Paul and his mother as he proudly takes her to Lincoln and she is proudly taken: nothing there, or even in the flower conversations, awkward as some of them are, needs special explanation—and the importance of glimpsing those powers having a bit of a surge is that we are able to pinpoint, *in the novel itself,* a possible source of dislocation, a source unaccommodated in it, and therefore possibly disturbing.

Disturbances are to be felt, it seems to me, all through part 2 of *Sons and Lovers.* Paul wonders about Miriam, loses his way, and circles round to try to find it again; the novel does much the same. An insoluble problem—a problem such as liking what you don't like—has been reached, a maze has been entered; various alleys are explored but found to be deadends, and the victim is freed only when the hedge is fed a very large dose of morphia and killed.

Typically, it is not action but thought that constitutes the interest of part 2. It's not what Miriam does, but what what she does means, that matters to Paul. I do not wish to be thought to be implying that a soliloquy, say, cannot "act" in a drama, that novels cannot be made out what characters think; the greatest dramas are, clearly, by great thinkers about great thinkers—for Hamlet and Lear are nothing if not great thinkers. But when we read, about Miriam, as Paul tells her they must separate, that

> she knew she felt in a sort of bondage to him, which she hated because she could not control it. She had hated her love for him from the moment it grew too strong for her. And, deep down, she had hated him because she loved him and he dominated her

not only is that hard to believe, from any evidence in the narrative, but the very language makes it doubtful. The violent attempt of the three "hated"s to induce conviction, the vulgar vagueness of "a sort of" and "deep down," and the indigestible paradox of "she had hated him because she loved him" all work to make us wonder if it is not anxiety rather than understanding that produces prose like this. Often enough, of course, Lawrence is calm enough, examining Paul's anxiety, holding it up for us to see:

> "What does she mean to me, after all? She represents something, like a bubble of foam represents the sea. But what is *she*? It's not her I care for." Then, startled by his own unconscious thoughts, that seemed to speak so distinctly that all the morning could hear, he undressed and ran quickly down the sands

and there is much, better than this, that distinguishes the writing in this part of the novel, much even in the entanglements of Paul and Miriam that are the understood entanglements of young lives, rather than the entanglements of a mind partly disabled from thinking about young lives, much that takes us clear of those entanglements altogether. But there remains a world of difference between the clarity and ease and good sense of this, say:

> There was always this feeling of jangle and discord in the Leivers family. Although the boys resented so bitterly this eternal appeal to their deeper feelings of resignation and proud humility, yet it had its effect on them. They could not establish between themselves and an outsider just the ordinary human feeling and unexaggerated friendship; they were always restless for the something deeper. Ordinary folk seemed shallow to them, trivial and inconsiderable. And so they were unaccustomed, painfully uncouth in the simplest social intercourse, suffering, and yet insolent in their superiority. Then beneath was the yearning for the soul-intimacy to which they could not attain because they were too dumb, and every approach to close connection was blocked by their clumsy contempt of other people. They wanted genuine intimacy, but they could not get even normally near to anyone, because they scorned to take the first steps, they scorned the triviality which forms common human intercourse

and this:

Now he realized that she had not been with him all the time, that her soul had stood apart, in a sort of horror. He was physically at rest, but no more. Very dreary at heart, very sad, and very tender, his fingers wandered over her face pitifully. Now again she loved him deeply. He was tender and beautiful.

"The rain!" he said.

"Yes—is it coming on you?" She put her hands over him, on his hair, on his shoulders, to feel if the raindrops fell on him. She loved him dearly. He, as he lay with his face on the dead pine-leaves, felt extraordinarily quiet. He did not mind if the raindrops came on him: he would have lain and got wet through: he felt as if nothing mattered, as if his living were smeared away into the beyond, near and quite lovable. This strange, gentle reaching-out to death was new to him.

This is not the expense of spirit in a waste of shame, not opposites held in one understanding as they are in that sonnet; it is opposites casually and even arbitrarily following one another, with death lowered from the flies at the end to negate all opposites, and as the representative, I suggest, of some obscure, unacknowledged feeling that nearly emerges in the following pages, where sex is linked with death, but in a fairly conventional way.

While recognizing Lawrence's inspired attempts (so often commented on) at capturing, even unsuccessfully, complex or evanescent states of being, we must nevertheless keep the right and capacity to distinguish between degrees of success, to say, for example, that he knows more than the Leivers boys know about themselves, but does not know more than Paul does, here. (Otherwise, for one thing, we might find it too easy to blame on Miriam what, despite occasional honourable but often clumsy authorial efforts at restoring a just balance between them, is perhaps rather more Paul's fault than it is hers.) It is even possible, I think, to see the whole Clara episode partly as a way of demonstrating that the lack of success in the earlier relationship was not Paul's fault—though to talk in terms of "faults" is to oversimplify what is at all times a complex business.

Love does not make anything whole for Paul. The transference of first love, mother love, is not successfully effected. With all his education, all his middle-class refinements, all his superior talents, all his distinguished individuality, all his thinking and reading and painting, he cannot manage it. It all fails him, all that consciousness, and it's really no surprise that—even though it's not in revenge for having made that failure inevitable—he kills its origin. But at the very end of the novel, he walks "towards the faintly humming, glowing town, quickly," and the "quickly" suggests that he is going towards life, towards light and movement. What it does not overtly say, or even suggest, is that he is going towards work, too.

Accounts of Lawrence the man suggest that in many ways he was quite like his father, and in particular in his delight in work. I like to think that in his own life Lawrence came closer to discovering what could help to make a whole of life than in *Sons and Lovers* he found. The evidence is there, it seems to me, in many pages through the novel, evidence that it is in their work that men and women make the most and the best of themselves, not in their love, that it is work that fulfils, that joins, that creates, that breaks barriers, that makes whole. One might even claim that the degree to which a character in *Sons and Lovers* works is the degree to which that character finds fulfilment. It is perhaps a poor lookout for love, which tends to begin where work ends, and towards the end of the novel Paul is coming closer to an understanding of this.

> "The night is free to you," he replied. "In the daytime I want to be by myself."
> "But why?" she said. "Why, even now, when we are on this short holiday?"
> "I don't know. Love-making stifles me in the daytime."

It stifles *Sons and Lovers* rather, too. But if the novel is about love, it is about work, too, and perhaps the survival of Walter Morel is a representation, in the complex art of the book, of the power of a lively force in it deeper than even Lawrence's understanding of the Morels and Bestwood quite reached.

Paul's Passion

Gavriel Ben-Ephraim

Paul abruptly turns toward sexuality, exaggerating its powers of redemption. The notion of passion as all-redeeming contradicts the
realized action of *Sons and Lovers,* and Paul claims therapeutic properties for sexuality that much of the novel belies. Though some fibre
of the bond between Gertrude and Walter Morel is never severed,
basically their story demonstrates that even a full sexual connection
cannot compensate for a lack of "finer intimacy." Paul denies this
when he discusses Gertrude with Miriam: "My mother, I believe,
got *real* joy and satisfaction out of my father at first. I believe she had
a passion for him; that's why she stayed with him. . . . That's what
one *must have,* I think . . . the real, real flame of feeling through
another person—once, only once, if it only lasts three months. See,
my mother looks as if she's *had* everything that was necessary for her
living and developing. There's not a tiny bit of feeling of sterility
about her. . . . Once it has happened to you, you can go on with
anything and ripen." Despite these incongruous comments, most of
Sons and Lovers testifies that Gertrude did not "ripen." Paul forgets
this because, having been divorced from passion, he inflates its
significance.

    The path he discovers to salvation seems delusory, but this is
not immediately apparent, and for a time Paul dedicates himself to
sexual experience. His powerful desires are embodied in the person

From *The Moon's Dominion: Narrative Dichotomy and Female Dominance in Lawrence's Earlier Novels.* ©1981 by Associated University Presses, Inc.

of Clara Dawes. Her female identity is firm and developed, as is communicated by her silent, womanly self-assurance, and by the erotic, nearly overripe, outlines of her body: "A certain heaviness, the heaviness of a very full ear of corn that dips slightly in the wind, that there was about her, made his brain spin." She replaces Walter as an embodiment of strong, sexual being and, accordingly, is frequently characterized by imagery of red. The color plays a role in many of her encounters with Paul; we note the rich earth of the river bank beside which they first consummate their relationship, and the "scarlet brick-red carnations" Paul buys Clara at the outset of this important excursion.

But Paul is too wounded by his past to emulate Walter's flame of achieved manhood and duplicate the sexual fulfillment of his parents' early period. Unable to come to Clara as an equal partner, he reverts to a mother-child relationship by apprehending her as a *magna mater* figure. She is perceived as a giantess, a great and overarching archetype of woman. Relatedly, the desire for self-annihilation Miriam felt in Paul becomes the essence of his love for Clara. Clara overwhelms Paul with a sense of self-reduction that recreates mother-infant proportions as it instances his obliteration by women: "He was Clara's white heavy arms, her throat, her moving bosom. That seemed to be himself. . . . There was no himself. The grey and black eyes of Clara, her bosom coming down on his, her arm that he held gripped between his hands, were all that existed. Then he felt himself small and helpless, her towering in her force above him."

Losing his being in a greater force, the body of woman or the universe itself, contains a suggestion of death. Scattering flowers over the kneeling Clara, at one point, Paul chants the grim old rhyme that begins "Ashes to ashes, dust to dust." Clara glances up at him with "pitiful, scared grey eyes," in a premonition of the death that is an inseparable part of his love. Indeed Paul often seems singled out for a tragic fate, a premature dying. (Most of the characters in *Sons and Lovers* are intimate with disease, physical or psychic, and with death by disease.) Yet to ephemerally "die" and dissolve into outer forces is not a purely negative matter, not indicative only of a pathology.

In Lawrence, as in the Romantic poets, loss of self is an extremely complex phenomenon; it may suggest rapturous transcendence, self-destruction, or both simultaneously. In his relationship with Clara Paul's problems lead (the connection is obscure but ines-capable) to supreme and liberating experiences of unity. The break in his being leaves an opening entered by the universe. Starting as less than a fully formed man, he can also become "more" than an individual. Paul seems to be one of those who are compensated for suffering and injury by capacities unavailable to ordinary people: he partakes of the paradox Edmund Wilson has described as "the con-ception of superior strength as inseparable from disability." Paul is thus capable of powerful fusion-experiences, at once erotic and mys-tical, that carry him and Clara into a principle of energy and sexual-ity far beyond their individual selves:

> Clara was not there for him, only a woman, warm, some-thing he loved and almost worshipped, there in the dark. But it was not Clara, and she submitted to him. The naked hunger and inevitability of his loving her, something strong and blind and ruthless in its primitiveness, made the hour almost terrible to her. She knew how stark and alone he was, and she felt it was great that he came to her; and she took him simply because his need was bigger either than her or him, and her soul was still within her. . . . What was she? A strong, strange, wild life, that breathed with his in the darkness through this hour. It was all so much bigger than themselves that he was hushed. They had met, and included in their meeting the thrust of the manifold grass-stems, the cry of the peewit, the wheel of the stars. . . . And after such an evening they both were very still, having known the immensity of passion. They felt small, half afraid, childish. . . . To know their own nothingness, to know the tremendous living flood which carried them always, gave them rest within themselves. If so great a magnificent power could overwhelm them, identify them altogether with itself, so that they knew they were only grains in the tremendous heave that lifted every grass-blade its little height, and every tree, and liv-ing thing, then why fret about themselves? They could let themselves be carried by life.

The passage brilliantly dramatizes ideas we think of as prototyp-ically Lawrencian. The notion that the most fulfilling lovemaking occurs in sympathetic relation to the living, surrounding universe comes vividly alive: Paul and Clara's experience of being carried away by the darkness contains the immensity critics have attributed to it. Yet there are problems within this very moving description: why does intuiting the hugeness and life of the universe cause a parallel intuition of individual "nothingness"? Apprehending the life around us does not enlarge the self, but diminishes it; going beyond taking pleasure in peaceful self-indifference, Paul finds satisfaction in self-cancellation. Why, we wonder, is this the manner of Paul's transcendence, and why does he present Clara, at last, with the sense of her own insignificance.

This self-diminishment leads to another problem in the encounter. Paul and Clara have merged with the universe but not with one another. We might say that theirs is a "higher" experience than the union of two people, yet Clara desires not the universe but a man. Though carried away by his desperation into the "tremendous living flood," Clara cannot be "satisfied" by their union. She is not content with apprehensions of the "tremendous heave that lifted every grass blade"; she wants what Miriam wanted, the human connection: "She had not got him; she was not satisfied. She had been there, but she had not gripped the—the something—she knew not what—which she was made to have." She turns to Paul for reassurance, wondering whether she is just a means for passional experience: "Is it *me* you want, or is it It?" The lack of personal emotion begins to ruin even their sex: "Gradually, some mechanical effort spoil their loving, or, when they had splendid moments, they had them separately and not so satisfactorily." The inhumanness takes its toll.

Lovemaking is not the end of his meetings with Clara: like Miriam she is a means to experiences of self-loss. Clara allows loss of self in sexuality, while Miriam encourages abandonment of self to her possessive spirituality. Both relationships create versions of Paul's original fusion with his mother; relatedly, Paul's merger-experiences with the universe can be viewed as a replacement for maternal engulfment. Paul's relationships with the two young women therefore recapitulate his primal attachment; Miriam and Clara function as substitutes, making Paul's eventual return to the maternal matrix inevitable.

Hence, it is not altogether surprising that Paul displaces some of his vexed emotions toward Gertrude onto Clara. Paul's intense and sentimental reactions toward Baxter Dawes constitute an equally coherent transference. More specifically, Paul displaces onto Clara and Baxter emotions toward his parents *he is unable himself to accept.*

In a man with Paul's background, hidden guilt toward his father, felt alongside hidden hostility toward his mother, would be natural. Part of the oedipal pattern is hatred toward the mother who keeps one in bondage and guilt towards the father whose woman one wants to "steal." (Indeed, a self-hating guilt toward the wronged father may explain Paul's frequent death wishes.) But in *Sons and Lovers* such feelings only surface indirectly—manifesting themselves in regard to the Dawes couple. This is one of the reasons why Clara and Baxter can legitimately be approached as surrogate parents for Paul. Indeed, a connection between the two couples is made in the text. When Paul describes the conflicts that had existed in the Daweses' marriage, Miriam notes the crucial parallel: "It was something like your mother and father."

Paul's "peculiar feeling of intimacy" towards Dawes, a man who is outwardly his enemy, can therefore be explained as a displacement of frustrated filial emotions. (Though weaker in character, on the surface Baxter is strikingly similar to Walter—both men are vital, rough, and incipiently brutal.) The parallel may also account for Paul's sudden release of Baxter after he succeeds in establishing a deadly hold on the larger man's throat during their fistfight over Clara. Not only might Paul relent out of some unconscious intimation of a symbolic parricide, but allowing Baxter to defeat and maul him is a playing out of a punishment ritual, a satisfaction of filial guilt feelings.

In relation to Clara and Baxter, Paul is enabled to reverse his habitual attitudes, and express the emotions and impulses repressed in his contacts with his actual parents. In the substitute relationship, Paul is sympathetic toward the man and hostile to the woman. The first faint sign of this reversal is Paul's odd reluctance to accept Clara's version of the marriage: " 'But why did you leave him?' . . . 'he sort of degraded me. He wanted to bully me because he hadn't got me. . . . And he seemed dirty.' 'I see.' He did not at all see. . . . 'But did you . . . ever give him a chance?' " After his violent encounter with Baxter, Paul's favorable view of him intensifies; when Dawes comes down with typhoid Clara, in another of the novel's feverish emotional transitions, also draws closer to him. She feels an enormous sense of guilt toward Baxter, though nothing in the novel contradicts her earlier estimate of him as a bullying, degrading man. There now takes place a justification of Baxter, a vilification of Clara. Abruptly, and without convincing actual or psychological cause, Clara almost revels in a guilt Paul corroborates: " 'I *have* been *vile* to him!' she said. 'I've said many a time you haven't treated him well,' he replied. . . . 'And I *made* him horrid—I know I did! You've taught me that. And he loved me a thousand times better than ever you do.' 'All right,' said Paul."

We are not informed of what actually took place during the Daweses' marriage, but observing the two characters in action it seems extraordinarily unlikely that their separation was entirely Clara's fault. Yet through Paul's accusations and Clara's self-recriminations the teller of the tale endeavors to convey such an impression. The narrator, then, working through various characters, communicates a subjective empathy for Baxter and a biased antagonism toward Clara. (We may speculate that Lawrence had his own repressed hostility toward women and sympathy toward men to release.) The Clara who is revealed to us by the tale is warm, insightful, and defiantly self-protective, while the tale's Baxter is loweringly hostile and dull-witted. At points, the narrator ignores these objectively demonstrated characteristics and places Clara in a position of inferiority, having her literally and figuratively kneel before Baxter. As in Miriam's case, the teller interferes with Clara's inner voice. Her thoughts and impulses toward Baxter grow increasingly discordant with her fundamental character. The distortion that results looks ahead to a problem that becomes common in Lawrence's later fiction: a woman submits to a man in a compliance that reverses our gradually formed impression of their relative strengths-of-being, so that the weaker character seems forced (by the narrator) into a dominating position. Thus, filled with her unexplained guilt, Clara suddenly bows to Dawes in a subservience that conflicts with the character as we know her: "She wanted to make restitution. . . . She wanted to humble herself to him, to kneel before him. She wanted now to be self-sacrificial. . . . She wanted to do penance. So she kneeled to Dawes, and it gave him a subtle pleasure."

I should not wish to be accused of simplification here. One of Lawrence's general achievements is his creation of characters who are open, flexible, and authentically self-contradictory. Certainly it is possible for Clara to have a momentary urge for self-prostration. But Clara's submission to Baxter culminates a process: it is a notably artificial fictional moment, but the whole sequence of which it is a part—describing the Paul-Clara-Baxter triangle—is comprised of willed and hollow occurrences. During this section of *Sons and Lovers* the author manipulates his dramatis personae, and there is an attenuation of the full, rendered life we expect, and receive, from the Lawrencian tale.

The novel returns to nearly its original force when Gertrude Morel returns to a central role within it. After Gertrude is stricken with cancer, Paul turns to her with passionate feelings of pity and adoration. He helps arrange a final reconciliation between Clara and Baxter, and is enabled to concentrate on the relationship that is most essential to him. The last scenes between Paul and Gertrude are love-scenes—the strangest the novel has to show: "His face was near hers. Her blue eyes smiled straight into his, like a girl's—warm, laughing with tender love. It made him pant with terror, agony and love." Now that it has been rendered harmless, they acknowledge their fearful bond: "They were both afraid of the veils that were ripping between them." At the same time, in the crucible of her dying feelings Gertrude is utterly unforgiving toward her husband: "Now she hated him. . . . She could not bear him to be in the room. And a few things, the things that had been most bitter to her, came up again so strongly that they broke from her, and she told her son." If this seems harshly vengeful, it also shows the depth of warping disillusionment she suffered from Walter.

Again, the hostility Paul has toward Gertrude is covert, emerging in the triangle, Paul-Clara-Baxter. But the young man's empathy toward his mother is dominant; the emotional cornerstone of *Sons and Lovers*. Therefore, tempting as it is to see Paul's mercy killing of his mother as liberating, a necessary euthanasia leading to his vitalization, there is no clear evidence that Paul frees himself from Gertrude at the end of the book. On the contrary, during the waning of her life they share a sickly death-intimacy. And while it is true that their painfully intense final intimacy does not preclude unconscious hostility to Gertrude on Paul's part, it is also undeniable that on the conscious, deliberate level he decides to take his mother's life because, in his unlimited empathy, he virtually shares her pain: "He knew the unutterable misery of her nights that would not go." It is an authentic case of killing with love.

After her death, he sees again the face that had always moved him, that had held his loyalty and love: "She lay like a girl asleep and dreaming of her love. The mouth was a little open, as if wondering from the suffering, but her face was young, her brow clear and white as if life had never touched it. He looked again at the eyebrows, at the small, winsome nose a bit on one side. She was young again."

Now, without her, his world comes undone: "His mother had really supported his life. . . . Now she was gone, and for ever behind him was the gap in life, the tear in the veil, through which his life seemed to drift slowly, as if he were drawn toward death. . . . His own hold on life was so unsure, because nobody held him [he was] feeling unsubstantial, shadowy." These lines forcefully testify to the disintegration of being Paul undergoes without his mother's support. The sense of purpose and coherence in life is lost without her: "There seemed no reason why people would walk along the street, and houses pile up in the daylight."

Still, there is ambiguity at the end of *Sons and Lovers,* communicated by the contradictory titles of the last two chapters: "The Release" and "Derelict." Which is it? Is Paul released from Gertrude at the end? If so, there is another ambivalency: is he released into life or death? Or is Paul now, in the sense of abandoned and directionless, "derelict?" Lawrence gives no simple answer, and Paul's fate becomes, as the many critical altercations about the matter show, a debatable question. Clearly, there is a tensile strength in Paul; he will not easily succumb: "He would not admit that he wanted to die, to have done. He would not own that life had beaten him, or that death had beaten him." Paul endures a fierce ontological struggle, but does not yield entirely to the forces of dissolution. He has inner resources: his artistic talent, a certain stubborn if delicate resiliency, a general capacity for survival. He looks outside his inner turmoil to the surrounding world. Small intimations of life come to him through the hopelessness: a donkey that nuzzles him under a "smoky red sunset," two mice scampering for food. He finds a life-force in the mechanical-industrial world, only regretting that he is not part of it: "Far away he could hear the sharp clinking of the trucks on the railway. No, it was not they that were far away. They were there in their places. But where was he himself?" This coincides with his earlier defense, to Clara, of industrial towns; he had argued that, for all its ugliness, the town will "come right."

But Paul's renewed life-urge takes its most serious form in a final search for a woman to save and restore him. He considers Clara first, but realizes she cannot accept the full responsibility of his despair: "Clara could not stand for him to hold on to. She wanted him, but not to understand him. He felt she wanted the man on top, not the real him that was in trouble." Surely, the answer to this is that he never offers Clara his "real" self; the inner man is absent from the relationship: "Even when he came to her he seemed unaware of her; always he was somewhere else." She prefers Baxter in the end, because he is *there;* however flawed, he is someone to encounter.

Paul then heads for the town, looking for hope in its gaslit lampposts. But the garish glare of the pubs gives him neither the escape his father finds in similar places nor a substitute for his mother's light. Within the pub he feels hopelessly alienated: "Everything suddenly stood back away from him. He saw the face of the barmaid, the gabbling drinkers, his own glass on the slopped, mahogany board, in the distance. There was something between him and them. He could not get into touch."

Finally, out of mounting desperation, he turns to the old relationship with Miriam. He is aware, as if for the first time, of her independent endurance. She seems the ideal person to save him; her spirituality now strikes him favorably: "She looked as if she had got something . . . some hope in heaven, if not in earth. . . . He would leave himself to her. She was better and bigger than he. He would depend on her." But she refuses to be his deliverance, to let him regress to this new form of infant/mother relation. Miriam concentrates on Paul's strength, not his weakness. She returns to her perennial encouragement of his creative work, his painting and drawing. "He felt again all her interest in his work. . . . Why was she always most interested in him as he appeared in his work?" Though sensing his silent need, she is unable to overwhelm him in his distress. She is accused, in these last pages, of wanting to smother Paul, to own him, but she is actually timorous, reticent. Miriam will not make the decision for him now, like a mother doing what is best for her child regardless of its will: "She had borne so long the cruelty of belonging to him and not being claimed by him. . . . She pleaded to him with all her love not to make it *her* choice."

Evidently, there are limitations to Miriam's possessive instincts, for she refuses to ingather the shattered man who comes to her for salvation. Paul wordlessly calls out to her to be stronger and more domineering than she ever was: to envelop him with surety and be more like Gertrude than Miriam. This is the "strong demand" of the "unknown thing in him"—the demand before which she is impotent. For in the moment of crisis, she cannot "take him and relieve him of the responsibility of himself," even if Paul wants "her to hold him and say, with joy and authority: 'Stop all this restlessness and beating against death. You are mine for a mate.'" Paul cannot take, he can only be taken. But Miriam's actions show her refusing to enfold Paul and be a mother to an annulled man.

Walking away from Miriam, Paul's last thoughts and feelings are rendered in a famous passage of astonishing beauty. Paul's fate, as anticipated in these final sentences, hovers perilously between being and nothingness, his soul caught between the beckoning extinguishing universe and the insistent continuous life of man.

> The town, as he sat upon the car, stretched away over the bay of the railway, a level fume of lights. Beyond the town the country, little smouldering spots for more towns—the sea—the night—on and on! And he had no place in it! Whatever spot he stood on, there he stood alone. From his breast, from his mouth, sprang the endless space, and it was there behind him, everywhere. The people hurrying along the streets offered no obstruction to the void in which he found himself. They were small shadows whose footsteps and voices could be heard, but in each of them the same night, the same silence. . . . Little stars shone high up; little stars spread far away in the flood-waters, a firmament below. Everywhere the vastness and terror of the immense night which is roused and stirred for a brief while by the day, but which returns, and will remain at last eternal, holding everything in its silence and its living gloom. There was no Time, only Space. Who could say his mother had lived and did not live? She had been in one place, and was in another; that was all. And his soul could not leave her, wherever she was. Now she was gone abroad into the night, and he was with her still. They were together. But yet there was his body, his chest, that leaned against the stile, his hands on the wooden bar. They seemed something. Where was he?—one tiny upright speck of flesh, less than an ear of wheat lost in the field. He could not bear it. On every side the immense dark silence seemed pressing him, so tiny a spark, into extinction, and yet, almost nothing, he could not be extinct. Night, in which everything was lost, went reaching out, beyond stars and sun. Stars and sun, a few bright grains, went spinning round for terror, and holding each other in

embrace, there in a darkness that outpassed them all, and left them tiny and daunted. So much, and himself, infinitesimal, at the core a nothingness, and yet not nothing.

"Mother!" he whispered—"mother!"

She was the only thing that held him up, himself, amid all this. And she was gone, intermingled herself. He wanted her to touch him, have him alongside with her.

But no, he would not give in. Turning sharply, he walked towards the city's gold phosphorescence. His fists were shut, his mouth set fast. He would not take that direction, to the darkness, to follow her. He walked towards the faintly, humming, glowing town, quickly.

This evocative statement conceives a dominating principle of death, eventually enfolding everyone in its blackness. Paul had been protected against this "immense dark silence" by the mother who fused with him into a whole and resisting unit. Since she has gone into the darkness, he seems destined to follow, his being inevitably drawn after hers. We realize that Paul's chance for survival is precisely equal to the degree of his differentiation from Gertrude. Having been one with her in life, it seems tragically probable that he will be one with her in death.

Still, we believe Lawrence when he tells us that Paul, so nearly nothing, is "yet not nothing." It would be altogether too fatalistic to deny Paul's capacity to defeat the past that has battered him so. Paul somehow maintains himself, the source of his strength mysteriously intertwined with his weakness.

But the last paragraph of the passage presents a problem, as it undercuts the tension and balance of the writing that precedes it. Having carefully described an annihilating universe, whose encroachments Paul is just barely able to withstand, the teller interposes lines that seem too entirely positive. Where the "endless space" had reduced all illumination to insignificance, the darkness is now countered with a power of light. Hence the "town" is given a potency at the end of the passage that is signally lacking from it at the beginning. More importantly, it is now suggested that Paul can triumph over the surrounding gloom absolutely, and that he can achieve the victory simply through an application of his defiant will.

We cannot say with certainty whether or not Paul will endure and escape the extinction that hangs over him. But we do know, contrary to the last paragraph of *Sons and Lovers,* that Paul Morel is too wounded and bereaved a young man to experience a beginning so hopeful and so new.

The Artist as Psychologist

Daniel J. Schneider

As Lawrence amplified and consolidated his vision of life, he continued to confront in his art the basic question that arose in his first two novels: How is it possible to lay bare the laws of psychic interaction without doing violence to life in its full concreteness and complexity? In *The Trespasser* he abstracts from the multifarious richness of experience those basic desires and fears that are eternally exhibited in the relationships between men and women. But to abstract "those principles and passions by which all minds are agitated" is to ignore "the streaks of the tulip," the variegated textures of ordinary life that elude schematization. *The Trespasser* is therefore a "pure" poem of the soul's elemental attractions and repulsions, a poetry of opposed symbols. Such a novel, excluding everything that might blur the focus on the elemental passions in conflict, lacks the mimetic density that an age of realism and naturalism has come to expect. It is too self-contained, too neat; and despite the symbolism's wide implications, the reader feels the confinement, the hothouse atmosphere of the prose poetry. Lawrence, perhaps intimidated by Ford Madox Ford's criticism of *The Trespasser,* turned from poetry to the sensuous realism of *Sons and Lovers.*

He had no intention of abandoning his efforts to define laws of psychology. In *Sons and Lovers,* as in *The Trespasser* and *The White Peacock,* he traces the subjugation of the male to the female, the obliteration of the male's selfhood and freedom as his soul is sucked up by Woman—either the spiritual woman or the possessive sensual woman. Indeed, Lawrence is interested in expanding his understanding of this subjugation to the love urge. By increasing the number of characters and by plotting his action over two generations, he gives himself the freedom to explore, above and beyond the oedipal problem, many variations of the more general problem that dominated his thinking during the period when he was struggling to "come through."

Early criticism of the novel, which focused on autobiographical content, on the oedipal problem, or on "destructive or counterfeit loves," tended to ignore the comprehensiveness of the pattern that Lawrence was tracing in the lives of his characters. Within the past decade, however, Richard Swigg and Stephen J. Miko have called attention to the more general pattern informing the action. Swigg, in his *Lawrence, Hardy, and American Literature,* points out that Lawrence was working with the struggle of life to rise "above the mass, above all the unconscious, formless, unresolved things which imprison [Paul's] developing 'on and on, nobody knows where.'" And Miko shrewdly observes that the novel focuses on the problem of how a "fundamental vitality can be embodied or released, what will restrict its growth, and what will encourage self-realization." I think this is exactly right: the pattern that Lawrence traces everywhere in *Sons and Lovers* is a pattern of life thwarted because of a person's subjugation to others or to capitalist society. Thus the novel reveals Lawrence's early meditations on the question that had become, by 1912, an obsession: how can the individual, single, separate, unique, enter into any relationship with other human beings and with society without sacrificing his individuality and without destroying his creative, purposive energies?

The conflict, at bottom, is not only between nature and culture but also between love and power, though Lawrence did not use the term "power" at this point in his life. The individual, motivated by an impulse to surrender himself to another person—and ultimately to the collective will of society—discovers that his sympathetic impulse, his love urge, threatens his very being as an individual. Paul's surrender to his mother cripples him and afflicts him with that "ontological insecurity," that fear of engulfment, which Marguerite Beede Howe views as the central concern of Lawrence's fiction. But all of the people in the novel are threatened by a kind of "engulfment" or by a thwarting of their potentialities as individuals. Howe's view that the novel exhibits the effort of an ontologically insecure hero to defend his ego against destruction and to return, through "uroboric incest," to the "state of grace from which we have fallen into the alienation of individuality" is psychoanalytically acceptable, but Lawrence was dealing not merely with the problem of his hero but with a more general problem that all people—both the secure and the insecure—confront in their relationships with others. To avoid the death of the soul, one must find a way to live in which the self is not absorbed or "nullified" by others or by society.

This idea is worked so strongly into all parts of the novel that one reads on to discover not only whether Paul will escape but also whether the others will be able to avoid the crippling effects of their love. All are well-meaning people; all are viewed naturalistically as innocent creatures thrown, through no fault of their own, into situations that "cramp" or "clog" or "block" or "imprison" their natural vitality. Indeed, the images in *Sons and Lovers,* issuing from the recurrent conflict between life and life constriction, fall into a simple pattern of oppositions. Life is quick, open, free, flowing, running, loose, alert, natural, easy, or spontaneous. When life is thwarted, it is gripped, held, clogged, tight, blind, tranced, cramped, slow, heavy, ill, hurt, awkward, unreal, bound, or imprisoned. These antinomies arise everywhere as Lawrence follows the fortunes of his characters; and the unique power and beauty of the novel are, to a large extent, the result of Lawrence's ability to move beyond superficial problems and to dramatize with directness and immediacy the underlying and fundamental human problem, which is ultimately the problem of almost all novels: our fear of the impairment of our life energies and of the thwarting of our deep desire to live fully and spontaneously, unimpeded by the pressures of society or of other people. Every one of Lawrence's characters faces not so much an immediate and practical problem as the fundamental "life issue"; and every one of them is seen both as a creature of possibilities—the heir or heiress of magnificent life—and as the victim of forces that suppress and poison the sacred fount.

The relationship of the father and mother—those unforgettably real and unforgettably archetypal figures—initiates the pattern of thwarted life and introduces the note of apprehension and dread that informs the entire novel. Both Morel and Gertrude, as we see with compassionate dread, are crippled by marriage and by the economic and social circumstances of their lives. Yet Morel, when he is alone, standing in what Lawrence might later have called "a proud noble selfhood," is vigorously alive. When Gertrude Coopard meets him, she watches him with fascination (as Miriam, later on, will watch Paul): "He was so full of colour and animation, his voice ran so easily into comic grotesque, he was so ready and so pleasant with everybody." His humor is "warm, a kind of gambolling." And the "sensuous flame of life . . . flowed off his flesh like the flame from a candle." Life runs and flows and flames in the man: these metaphors are recurrent in this novel. Morel rises early, piles "a big fire," and sits down "to an hour of joy"; alone, he is "happy." Being natural and healthy, he loves nature, and his vitality is not daunted even by the mine: "He loved the early morning, and the walk across the field. So he appeared at the pit-top, often with a stalk from the hedge between his teeth, which he chewed all day to keep his mouth moist, down the mine, feeling quite as happy as he was in the field." Again, Lawrence stresses that Morel is quick with the quick of life: "As she heard him sousing heartily in cold water, heard the eager scratch of the steel comb on the side of the bowl, as he wetted his hair, she closed her eyes in disgust. As he bent over, lacing his boots, there was a certain vulgar gusto in his movements that divided him from the reserved, watchful rest of the family." His spontaneous life energy is most sharply realized when he is working, fulfilling his deep male creative desires. Hammering the glowing iron on his "goose," Morel is "jolly." He sings, too, when he mends boots "because of the jolly sound of the hammering"; he is happy mending his pit trousers, happy when he makes fuses, and happy when, in his "warm way," he tells stories about the pit, about the horse Taffy and the mice that somehow thrive in the darkness.

But the spontaneous life of the man, however robust, cannot continue to flow under these circumstances. If the pits do not kill him, they cripple him; and his "wonderfully young body, muscular, without any fat," bears "too many blue scars, like tattoo-marks, where the coal-dust remained under the skin." But the deepest crippling occurs, of course, in his marriage. Cast off by his wife and children, he becomes "more or less a husk"; "he could not live in that atmosphere"; and he falls into "a slow ruin." Indeed, "his body . . . shrank," and the contraction of his life prepares obliquely for the life constriction to be repeated in his son's life. What Gertrude does to Morel, Miriam will do to Paul.

The pattern of thwarted life is continued in Lawrence's handling of Mrs. Morel. At the outset Lawrence tells us that her life is "baffled and gripped into incandescence by thought and spirit," but the truth is that Mrs. Morel, like her husband, is very richly alive when she is not being suffocated by her husband's presence. Indeed, Lawrence takes pains to emphasize her quickness and vitality:

> She spat on the iron, and a little ball of spit bounded, raced off the dark, glossy surface. Then, kneeling, she rubbed the iron on the sack lining of the hearth-rug vigorously. She was warm in the ruddy firelight. Paul loved the way she crouched and put her head on one side. Her movements were light and quick. It was always a pleasure to watch her.

Her vitality is manifested in a number of ways. She loves her marketing, and when she returns "triumphant," her "step in the entry" is a "quick light step." She rejoices in the florists in Nottingham and exclaims at the abundance and beauty of the fuchsias. Paul sees her face as "bright with living warmth," and he draws from her "the life-warmth, the strength to produce." To the end of her life, when she is dying of cancer, Mrs. Morel responds with enthusiasm to living things: "'Anna,' she exclaimed, 'I saw a lizard out on that rock!' Her eyes were so quick; she was still so full of life." Looking out of the window, she cries, "'There are my sunflowers!'" In all these passages, she is anything but "baffled and gripped into incandescence by thought and spirit." She is as joyfully alive as her husband is, but only when she is apart from him.

Her contraction, her "clogging," occurs because of her middle-class ambition and their poverty. "Her still face, with the mouth closed tight from suffering and disillusion and self-denial, and her nose the smallest bit on one side, and her blue eyes so young, quick, and warm, made [Paul's] heart contract with love. When she was quiet, so, she looked brave and rich with life, but as if she had been done out of her rights." In her disillusionment, she turns the children against their father; all become "reserved, watchful," and "hushed" as the miner enters the house. The years of battling create in her a "hardness." Her mouth is "always closed with disillusion," and as she grows frail, her face and eyes are "fixed, reflecting the relentlessness of life." So her only hope in life is that her sons will do great things.

All of the children are deeply affected by the tension between the parents, and the imagery defining the effects of the parental strife is built upon the basic pattern of the contrast between life and life constriction. When they are very young, they lie abed "with their hearts in the grip of an intense anguish." Their father is "like the scotch in the smooth, happy machinery of the house," and when he enters, there is a "fall of silence," "the shutting off of life."

Very deliberately, Lawrence works with imagery of quickness and constraint. William as a boy "could run like the wind"; his face is "extraordinarily mobile. Usually he looked as if he saw things, was full of life, and warm; then his smile, like his mother's, came suddenly and was very lovable, and then, when there was any clog in his soul's quick running, his face went stupid and ugly." The conflict within him when he becomes engaged to Gipsy makes him "unnatural and intense"; his health fails; he dies of erysipelas.

Arthur, too, is quick—"a quick, careless, impulsive boy, a good deal like his father"; he is "full of life," but his "fiery temper" becomes "uncertain" as he grows older. He enlists in the army; then he marries; and he is "caught": "It did not matter how he kicked and struggled, he was fast," "he belonged to his wife and child." The imagery of bondage and imprisonment occurs everywhere in this novel, and Arthur is but one of many whose natural life and freedom are violated by society.

Lawrence's handling of Paul follows the pattern already established. Even though Lawrence suggests, shortly after Paul's birth, that this infant, who "boiled" in his mother's womb, has been "stunned" at "some point in its soul," though Lawrence emphasizes that the damage to Paul's vitality has been done before birth and notes "the peculiar knitting of the baby's brows, and the peculiar heaviness of its eyes, as if it were trying to understand something that was pain," though there is this very deliberate preparation for his later difficulties, Paul is, in truth, like the other children, quick and full of life. Annie, we learn, "raced wildly at lerky with the other young wild-cats of the Bottoms. And always Paul flew beside her." Like his father, Paul "loved being out in the country," and he "scoured the coppices and woods and old quarries, as long as a blackberry was to be found." As a lad, he is "quick, light, graceful"; "his eyes were quick and bright with life." He responds eagerly to others: the Leivers "kindled him and made him glow to his work," and "he worked all through hay-harvest with them." His tread is always "quick and firm"; he jumps up; he exclaims; when he mounts the swing, "every bit of him" goes "swinging, like a bird that swoops for joy of movement"; "it was almost as if he were a flame that had lit a warmth in [Miriam] whilst he swung in the middle air." In his youthful gusto, he asserts that Mary Queen of Scots did not deserve imprisonment because "she was only lively." And when he paints, it is life that he wants to capture: "the shimmering protoplasm in the leaves and everywhere, and not the stiffness of the shape. That seems dead to me. Only this shimmeriness is the real living."

All the images of life blockage mark the dreadful threat to this soul, and most prominent are those of imprisonment, immobility, and stillness. When he goes to collect his father's wages, he is "jammed behind the legs of the men," "pushed against the chimney-piece." " 'They always stan' in front of me, so's I can't get out,' " he complains to his mother. When he applies for the job at Jordan's, he is again threatened by entrapment. On the way to Jordan's, he feels "something screwed up tight inside him." Entering the factory, he passes "under the archway, as into the jaws of the dragon," and except for the yard, "the place was like a pit." In the interview, words refuse to come; he stammers and is "stuck." Yet, like his father, he brings his flaming vitality into this pit, and we learn that he "always enjoyed it when the work got faster."

His natural environment seems to be the motion of life. But when he meets Miriam, a serious threat to his vitality appears. He seeks the girl out "as if for nourishment. Together they seemed to sift the vital fact from an experience." But seeking nourishment, he is slowly starved. Miriam, the "maiden in bondage," is "gripped tight" or "in a trance"; she is afraid to move, her body is "not flexible and living." "There was no looseness or abandon about her. Everything was gripped stiff with intensity." She "held herself in a grip"; her face is "blind" or "closed." Ashamed of her desire for Paul, she is "tied" to "a stake of torture," her soul "coiled into knots of shame." And so she makes Paul feel "anxious and imprisoned." " 'She is one of those who will want to suck a man's soul out till he has none of his own left,' " Paul's mother warns. And gradually "his natural fire of love" is "transmitted into the fine stream of thought"; she "killed the joy and warmth in him"; she "spoilt his ease and naturalness." Forcing Paul to be "spiritual," she threatens to destroy the young man as Gertrude has destroyed Morel. Paul is split in two, "unable to move." After he and Miriam make love, "life seemed a

shadow, day a white shadow; night and death, and stillness, and inaction, this seemed like *being*. To be alive, to be urgent and insistent—that was *not-to-be*." It is not until he leaves Miriam, securing
"three days that were all his own," that the life energy returns: "It
was sweet to rush through the morning lanes on his bicycle." Like
his father, he can live only when he is freed of the incubus of the
spiritual woman.

Clara Dawes, when Paul meets her, is another person whose
natural vitality has been impaired. She has left Baxter Dawes because
"it's a question of living. With him, she was only half-alive; the rest
was dormant, deadened." Condemned to daily toil at her spinning
jenny, Clara is a woman in bondage: "Her arm moved mechanically,
that should never have been subdued to a mechanism, and her head
was bowed to the lace." Her eyes look "dumb with humiliation,
pleading with a kind of captive misery." But Lawrence suggests that
Clara, like Miriam and like Gertrude, also threatens to suck up Paul's
soul—to awaken herself by drawing upon his vitality. She sees him
as "a vigorous slender man, with exhaustless energy"; his eyes
"seemed to dance." Although for a time Paul's love for Clara gives
him life and motion ("he raced her down the road to the green turf
bridge. She could run well. The colour soon came, her throat was
bare, her eyes shone. He loved her for being so luxuriously heavy,
and yet so quick," and although their passion, too, brings life (they
are swept up in a "tremendous living flood which carried them always"), Clara presently seeks to get him, to "absorb" him. And Paul
must shake her off: "He preferred to be alone. She made him feel
imprisoned when she was there, as if he could not get a free deep
breath, as if there were something on top of him. She felt his desire
to be free of her." So, like his father, he must escape the prison of
suffocation. Should he fail to break free, he may become, like his
father, "small and mean."

There remains for Paul the problem of escaping from his
mother. Although he has drawn the life warmth from her, he sees
her as preventing his free development: "Sometimes he hated her,
and pulled at her bondage. His life wanted to free itself of her. It was
like a circle where life turned back on itself, and got no further. . . .
He could not be free to go forward with his own life." As *The Rainbow* develops the theme of escape from confining circles, so Lawrence here begins to introduce that theme of Emersonian expansion
outward toward the infinite. Paul wants "maximum of being"; but

as his mother dies, he is afflicted in much the same way as he was after making love to Miriam: "The realest thing was the thick darkness at night. That seemed to him whole and comprehensible and restful. . . . He wanted every thing to stand still, so that he could be with [his mother] again." Motion and life fill him with "a flame of agony." "He did not want to move." Again, when he meets Miriam, he sees that "a sort of stiffness, almost of woodenness, had come upon her," and he tells her that he "should die there [in Miriam's pocket] smothered." So, he is left, at the end, both craving and not craving death. But his final decision—to turn back to the "glowing town"—is the decision for life against death, and the imagery associated with the town suggests that it is the seat of life. Appropriately, in a novel that has everywhere dramatized the struggle of life against all that threatens to block and thwart human beings, the final word is "quickly."

The novel is not without its defects. Paul is so intensely alive, alert, observant, and quick, in a dozen different scenes, that one cannot help feeling uneasy about his neurotic behavior in the last chapters of the novel. Julian Moynahan's uneasiness about a conflict between a sort of Freudian determinism that is implicit in Paul's "drift toward death" and an "indeterminate" vitalism that permits Paul to turn back to the "glowing town" seems to me justified. Stephen J. Miko's reply to Moynahan is that "the vital system is at bottom more fundamental than the pattern of fixation which Moynahan cogently spells out" (*Toward* Women in Love); but this defense cannot stand up unless one can demonstrate that Paul's neurotic behavior arises through probability and necessity. But Paul's behavior does not seem inevitable. Lawrence does not convincingly establish that Paul's mother, who has disappeared from the novel during much of its second half, is the "one place in the world that stood solid and did not melt into unreality." Trusting the tale and not the teller, one must conclude that Paul's psychic paralysis, even though thematically appropriate, is not adequately prepared for and is to a degree made implausible by the vivid representations of his vigorous life. Further, it is hard to accept that Gertrude's death would necessarily cause Paul's psychic injury because Lawrence does not build into the novel the sort of action that would lead conclusively to that result: the only adequate test of Paul's oedipal problem would have been to confront him with a woman who, unlike Miriam and Clara, was well suited to him, thus showing that he could not love even the right woman.

Again, Lawrence's judgment of Morel—"He had denied the God in him"—understandably disturbs one critic (Scott Sanders). This judgment is apparently contradicted by the observation that Mrs. Morel, "seeking to make him nobler than he could be, . . . destroyed him." Here we confront one of the great problems that Lawrence had to solve in adjusting his psychology to his art. From the point of view of Lawrence the psychologist, Morel is innocent: he cannot be condemned for being what he is and what Gertrude and the mines have made him. From the point of view of the religious artist, Morel is guilty: like Siegmund in *The Trespasser,* Morel fails to strive beyond himself. But Lawrence cannot have it both ways. In a novel in which, as Stephen Miko notes, there is "curiously little moral judgment by the author" (*Toward* Women in Love), the judgment of Morel arises from premises that lie outside the novel— the Nietzschean idea of the nobility of the higher man or the vitalist idea of aspiration and striving. The technical problem that Lawrence faces is that of grounding moral judgments in the innocence of life. Instead of imposing judgments, he has to make them arise from life itself, life as experienced by each individual. I shall examine his solution to this problem in *The Rainbow.*

Looking back over *Sons and Lovers,* one can see how richly it carries out the theme that Anais Nin calls central in Lawrence: the theme of "livingness." The achievement of "maximum of being" is possible only when the individual maintains his proud selfhood, asserting, "I am I." All connections with others lead to a cramping or contraction of the soul. Yet Lawrence knows that connection with other human beings, and with Being Itself, is essential to one's fullest development. The problem, the central problem in all of his work, is indeed to "connect" with other life (ultimately with the cosmos) and still to remain uncompromised in the depths of the soul. Paul Morel has a keen sense of the possibilities of life; he knows that he can do great things if he acts on his soul's wisdom. But Paul is Gertrude's son and, like Hamlet, is betrayed in his love for his mother. Like Hamlet, too, he sees that men everywhere are destroyed by their blind submission to society or to lovers who violate their souls. To fall in love—even to love one's neighbor—is to love one's enemy, who cripples and immobilizes the soul.

In *Sons and Lovers* Paul seeks "nourishment" in three women, and his spontaneous life is threatened by each. The problem of loving and yet retaining one's individuality is not solved in this novel;

Lawrence had to write six other novels to define to his own satisfaction the vital relationships between man and woman, man and man, and man and the cosmos that would ensure fullest connection while allowing fullest integrity. But in *Sons and Lovers*—this early definition of the central problem—Lawrence discovers the materials he needs in order to dramatize, with maximum apprehension and dread, the threat to the spontaneous life of the individual. In the context of ordinary life and of utter domesticity, in the mines that symbolize the industrial world and in middle-class respectability, he discovers the causes of the death of the soul.

Chronology

1885	David Herbert Lawrence born September 11 in Eastwood, a Nottingham mining village, the fourth child of Arthur Lawrence, a coal miner, and Lydia Beardsall Lawrence, a former schoolteacher of lower-middle-class background.
1898–1901	Attends Nottingham High School on a County Council Scholarship.
1901	Meets Jessie Chambers, who becomes his childhood amour and the model for Miriam Leivers of *Sons and Lovers;* works for a dealer in artificial limbs.
1902–6	Becomes pupil-teacher at British School at Eastwood; begins writing *The White Peacock* and poems. Engaged to Jessie Chambers.
1906–8	Attends Nottingham University College, taking the teacher's certificate course.
1908–11	Teaches at the Davidson Road Boy's School. Jessie Chambers sends some of Lawrence's poems to Ford Madox Hueffer's *English Review,* where Lawrence's poetry is first published in the November 1909 issue. Friendship with Helen Corke, a schoolteacher.
1910	Starts writing *The Trespasser;* engagement with Jessie broken off; starts writing *Paul Morel* (to become *Sons and Lovers*). His mother dies of cancer, December 10.
1911	His first novel, *The White Peacock,* is published by Heinemann in January.
1912	Falls ill and gives up teaching. Introduced to Frieda von Richthofen Weekley, the thirty-two-year-old

155

wife of his former French professor at University College, Nottingham. *The Trespasser* published in May. Lawrence and Frieda elope, traveling together in Germany and Italy. Finishes *Sons and Lovers;* writes plays, stories, and poems.

1913   *Sons and Lovers* published in May. *The Insurrection of Miss Houghton* (to become *The Lost Girl*) begun. Works on draft of *The Sisters* (to become *Women in Love* and *The Rainbow*); writes tales published as *The Prussian Officer* (1914). Meets John Middleton Murry.

1914   Frieda divorces Weekley and marries Lawrence. *Study of Thomas Hardy* written; continues work on *The Sisters.*

1915   *The Rainbow* published in September, suppressed for "indecency" in November. Writes *The Crown.*

1916   Lives in Cornwall; finishes writing *Women in Love.*

1917   Denied passport to U.S.; rejected as medically unfit for military service; expelled by military from Cornwall on suspicion of spying.

1918   Drafts *Movements in European Literature,* the play *Touch and Go,* and *The Fox.*

1919   Writes tales published as *England, My England;* drafts *Aaron's Rod;* returns to Continent: Florence, Capri, Taormina.

1920   *Women in Love* is privately printed in New York. Completes and publishes *The Lost Girl;* writes *Birds, Beasts and Flowers, Psychoanalysis and the Unconscious* (1921), and a novel, *Mr. Noon.*

1921   Writes *Fantasia of the Unconscious* (1922), *The Captain's Doll,* and *The Ladybird.*

1922   Visits Ceylon and Australia, where he writes most of *Kangaroo. Aaron's Rod* published in April. Takes up residence in Taos, New Mexico.

1923   Completes and publishes *Birds, Beasts and Flowers; Kangaroo* published; begins work on *The Plumed Serpent.* Visits Mexico and Europe.

1924   Writes *Mornings in Mexico* (1927), *St. Mawr* (1925), and the tales *The Princess* and *The Woman Who Rode Away.*

1925   Completes *The Plumed Serpent* and publishes the play *David*.

1926   *The Plumed Serpent* published in January. Takes up residence near Florence. Begins writing *Lady Chatterley's Lover*.

1927   Begins work on *Escaped Cock* (published as *The Man Who Died*) and *Etruscan Places* (1932).

1928   Completes *Lady Chatterley's Lover*, published first in Florence, though numerous pirated editions appear in England. Resides in South of France. Postal authorities seize manuscript of *Pansies*. Completes *The Man Who Died* (1929).

1929   Police raid exhibition of Lawrence's paintings at the Warren Gallery, London (July). Writes *More Pansies, Pornography and Obscenity, Apocalypse,* and *Nettles*.

1930   Dies of tuberculosis at a sanatorium near Antibes, France, on March 2.

1960   Penguin Books publishes unexpurgated *Lady Chatterley's Lover* in England and is prosecuted under the Obscene Publications Act. After a celebrated trial, Penguin wins.

Contributors

HAROLD BLOOM, Sterling Professor of the Humanities at Yale University, is the author of *The Anxiety of Influence, Poetry and Repression,* and many other volumes of literary criticism. His forthcoming study, *Freud: Transference and Authority,* attempts a full-scale reading of all of Freud's major writings. A MacArthur Prize Fellow, he is general editor of five series of literary criticism published by Chelsea House. During 1987–88, he served as Charles Eliot Norton Professor of Poetry at Harvard University.

DOROTHY VAN GHENT taught at Kansas University and the University of Vermont. Her numerous publications include *The English Novel: Form and Function* and *Keats: The Myth of the Hero.*

H. M. DALESKI, Professor of English Literature at the Hebrew University of Jerusalem, is the author of *The Forked Flame: A Study of D. H. Lawrence, Dickens and the Art of Analogy,* and *Joseph Conrad: The Way of Dispossession.*

LOUIS L. MARTZ, Sterling Professor Emeritus of English at Yale University, is the author of *The Poetry of Meditation, The Paradise Within, The Poem of the Mind, The Wit of Love,* and *Poet of Exile.*

CALVIN BEDIENT is Professor of English at the University of California at Los Angeles and the author of *Architects of the Self* and *Eight Contemporary Poets.*

DANIEL R. SCHWARZ is Professor of English at Cornell University. He is the author of *Disraeli's Fiction, Conrad: Almayer's Folly to Under Western Eyes* and *The Humanistic Heritage.*

MARK KINKEAD-WEEKES is Professor of English at the University of Kent at Canterbury and the author of *Samuel Richardson: Dramatic Novelist*.

E. P. SHRUBB is Senior Lecturer in English at the University of Sydney.

GAVRIEL BEN-EPHRAIM teaches at Tel Aviv University and is the author of *The Moon's Dominion: Narrative Dichotomy and Female Dominance in the First Five Novels of D. H. Lawrence*.

DANIEL J. SCHNEIDER is Professor of English at the University of Tennessee at Knoxville and the author of books on Lawrence and Henry James.

Bibliography

Adamowski, T. H. "The Father of All Things: The Oral and the Oedipal in *Sons and Lovers.*" *Mosaic* 14, no. 4 (1981): 69–88.

Albright, Daniel. "D. H. Lawrence." In *Personality and Impersonality: Lawrence, Woolf and Mann.* Chicago: University of Chicago Press, 1978.

Alinei, Tamara. "Three Times Morel: Recurrent Structure in *Sons and Lovers.*" *Dutch Quarterly Review of Anglo-American Letters* 5 (1975): 39–53.

Alldritt, Keith. *The Visual Imagination of D. H. Lawrence.* Evanston, Ill.: Northwestern University Press, 1971.

Balbert, Peter H. "Forging and Feminism: *Sons and Lovers* and the Phallic Imagination." *The D. H. Lawrence Review* 11 (1978): 93–113.

Baldanza, Frank. "*Sons and Lovers:* Novel to Film as a Record of Cultural Growth." *Literature/Film Quarterly* 1, no. 1 (1973): 64–70.

Beal, Anthony, ed. *D. H. Lawrence: Selected Literary Criticism.* New York: Viking, 1956.

Beards, Richard D. "*Sons and Lovers* as Bildungsroman." *College Literature* 1 (1974): 204–17.

Bloom, Harold, ed. *Modern Critical Views: D. H. Lawrence.* New Haven, Conn.: Chelsea House, 1986.

Buckley, Jerome H. "D. H. Lawrence: The Burden of Apology." In *Season of Youth: The Bildungsroman from Dickens to Golding.* Cambridge: Harvard University Press, 1974.

Burgess, Anthony. *Flame Into Being: The Life and Work of D. H. Lawrence.* New York: Arbor House, 1985.

Burwell, Rose Marie. "Schopenhauer, Hardy, and Lawrence: Toward a New Understanding of *Sons and Lovers.*" *Western Humanities Review* 28 (1974): 105–17.

Callow, Philip. *Son and Lover: The Young Lawrence.* London: Bodley Head, 1975.

Clark, L. D. *The Minoan Distance: The Symbolism of Travel in D. H. Lawrence.* Tucson: University of Arizona Press, 1980.

Clarke, Colin. *River of Dissolution: D. H. Lawrence and English Romanticism.* New York: Barnes & Noble, 1969.

Daleski, H. M. *The Forked Flame: A Study of D. H. Lawrence.* Evanston, Ill.: Northwestern University Press, 1965.

Farr, Judith, ed. *Twentieth Century Interpretations of* Sons and Lovers: *A Collection of Critical Essays*. Englewood Cliffs, N.J.: Prentice-Hall, 1970.

Gomme, A. H., ed. *D. H. Lawrence: A Critical Study of the Major Novels and Other Writings*. New York: Barnes & Noble, 1978.

Hamalian, Leo, ed. *D. H. Lawrence: A Collection of Criticism*. New York: McGraw-Hill, 1973.

Hampson, Carolyn. "The Morels and the Gants: Sexual Conflict as a Universal Theme." *Thomas Wolfe Review* 8, no. 1 (1984): 27–40.

Hoffman, F. J., and H. T. Moore, eds. *The Achievement of D. H. Lawrence*. Norman: University of Oklahoma Press, 1953.

Kazin, Alfred. "Sons, Lovers and Mothers." *Partisan Review* 29 (1962): 373–85.

Littlewood, J. C. F. "Lawrence and the Scholars." *Essays in Criticism* 33 (1983): 175–86.

MacLeod, Sheila. *Lawrence's Men and Women*. London: Heinemann, 1985.

Mandell, G. P. *The Phoenix Paradox: A Study of Renewal Through Change in the "Collected Poems" and "Last Poems" of D. H. Lawrence*. Carbondale: Southern Illinois University Press, 1984.

Meyers, Jeffrey, ed. *D. H. Lawrence and Tradition*. Amherst: University of Massachusetts Press, 1985.

Moore, Harry T., ed. *A D. H. Lawrence Miscellany*. Carbondale: Southern Illinois University Press, 1959.

Moynahan, Julian, ed. Sons and Lovers: *Text, Background and Criticism*. New York: Viking, 1968.

Murfin, Ross C. *The Poetry of D. H. Lawrence: Texts and Contexts*. Lincoln: University of Nebraska Press, 1983.

Nehls, Edward H., ed. *D. H. Lawrence: A Composite Biography*. 3 vols. Madison: University of Wisconsin Press, 1957–59.

Panken, Shirley. "Some Psychodynamics in Sons and Lovers: A New Look at the Oedipal Theme." *Psychoanalytic Review* 61 (1974): 571–89.

Phillips, Danna. "Lawrence's Understanding of Miriam through Sue." *Recovering Literature: A Journal of Contextualist Criticism* 7, no. 1 (1979): 46–56.

Sagar, Keith. *The Art of D. H. Lawrence*. Cambridge: Cambridge University Press, 1966.

Salgado, Giamini, ed. *D. H. Lawrence:* Sons and Lovers. *A Casebook*. London: Macmillan, 1969.

Schneider, Daniel J. *The Consciousness of D. H. Lawrence: An Intellectual Biography*. Lawrence: University Press of Kansas, 1986.

Schorer, Mark. "Technique as Discovery." *Hudson Review* 1 (Spring 1948): 67–87.

Spector, Judith. "Taking Care of Mom: Erotic Degradation, Dalliances, and Dichotomies in the Works of Just About Everyone." *The Sphinx: A Magazine of Literature and Society* 4, no. 3 (1981): 184–201.

Spilka, Mark, ed. *D. H. Lawrence: A Collection of Critical Essays*. Englewood Cliffs, N.J.: Prentice-Hall, 1963.

Taylor, John A. "The Greatness in Sons and Lovers." *Modern Philology* 71 (1973/74): 380–87.

Tedlock, E. W., ed. *D. H. Lawrence and* Sons and Lovers: *Sources and Criticism.* New York: New York University Press, 1965.

Van Tassel, Daniel E. "The Search for Manhood in D. H. Lawrence's *Sons and Lovers.*" *Costerus* 3 (1972): 197–210.

Worthen, John. *D. H. Lawrence and the Idea of the Novel.* London: Macmillan, 1979.

Acknowledgments

"On *Sons and Lovers*" by Dorothy Van Ghent from *The English Novel: Form and Function* by Dorothy Van Ghent, © 1953 by Dorothy Van Ghent. Reprinted by permission.

"The Son and the Artist" (originally entitled "The Release: The First Period") by H. M. Daleski from *The Forked Flame: A Study of D. H. Lawrence* by H. M. Daleski, © 1965 by H. M. Daleski. Reprinted by permission.

"Portrait of Miriam" by Louis L. Martz from *Imagined Worlds: Essays on Some English Novels and Novelists in Honour of John Butt,* edited by Maynard Mack and Ian Gregor, © 1968 by Methuen & Co., Ltd. Reprinted by permission.

"The Vital Self" by Calvin Bedient from *Architects of the Self* by Calvin Bedient, © 1972 by the Regents of the University of California. Reprinted by permission of the University of California Press.

"Speaking of Paul Morel: Voice, Unity, and Meaning in *Sons and Lovers*" by Daniel R. Schwarz from *Studies in the Novel* 8, no. 3 (Fall 1976), © 1976 by North Texas State University. Reprinted by permission.

"Eros and Metaphor in *Sons and Lovers*" (originally entitled "Eros and Metaphor: Sexual Relationships in the Fiction of Lawrence") by Mark Kinkead-Weekes from *Lawrence and Women,* edited by Anne Smith, © 1978 by Vision Press Ltd. Reprinted by permission.

"Reading *Sons and Lovers*" by E. P. Shrubb from *Sydney Studies in English* 6 (1980–81), © 1981 by E. P. Shrubb. Reprinted by permission.

"Paul's Passion" (originally entitled "The Underlying Pattern: *Sons and Lovers*") by Gavriel Ben-Ephraim from *The Moon's Dominion: Narrative Dichotomy and Female Dominance in Lawrence's Earlier Novels* by Gavriel Ben-Ephraim, © 1981 by Associated University Presses, Inc. Reprinted by permission of Associated University Presses, Inc.

"The Artist as Psychologist" (originally entitled "Psychology and Art in the Early Novels") by Daniel J. Schneider from *D. H. Lawrence: The Artist as Psychologist* by Daniel J. Schneider, © 1984 by the University Press of Kansas. Reprinted by permission of the University Press of Kansas.

Index

Adam Bede (George Eliot), 12
"Adolf," 25
Art of D. H. Lawrence, The (Sagar), 1
"At a Loose End," 78
Austen, Jane, 71

Beatrice, 65, 89
Blake, William, 26

Chambers, Jessie, 1, 80–81; *Sons and Lovers* as viewed by, 37, 38, 74
Chesterton, G. K., 71
Collier's Friday Night, A, 25
Corke, Helen, 37

Dawes, Baxter: Clara Dawes's relationship to, 135–36, 139, 150; general characteristics of, 94, 113–14, 135, 136; Paul Morel's relationship to, 4, 134, 135
Dawes, Clara: Baxter Dawes's relationship to, 135–36, 139, 150; general characteristics of, 85, 100, 116–17, 132, 135–36, 150; Gertrude Morel's relationship to, 36, 58, 98, 150; Miriam Leivers compared to, 98, 99, 100, 150; as mother figure, 132, 135; Paul Morel's relationship to, 7, 15, 19, 74, 75, 76, 83, 97, 98–100, 106–7, 121, 132–34, 138–39; sexuality of, 132, 133; vitality of, 100, 136, 150
D. H. Lawrence: A Composite Biography (Nehls, ed.), 1, 2

D. H. Lawrence: A Personal Record (Chambers), 1
D. H. Lawrence Miscellany, A (Moore, ed.), 1
D. H. Lawrence: Reminiscences and Correspondence (Brewster), 23
Dickens, Charles, 71
Draper, R. P., 36

Eliade, Mircea, 77
Eliot, George, 71
"End of Another Home Holiday," 36

Fantasia of the Unconscious, 43, 94
Fergusson, Francis, 6, 8
Fielding, Henry, 11–12
Ford, Ford Madox, 143
Forster, E. M., 71
Freud, Sigmund, 1, 33, 74–75

Garnett, Edward, 1, 34, 101
Gipsy. *See* Western, Louisa Lily Denys

Hamlet (Shakespeare), 123, 125–26, 152
Hardy, Thomas, 1, 12, 71
Heretics (Chesterton), 71
Hoffman, Frederick J., 33
Hough, Graham, 39
Howe, Marguerite Beede, 144–45

Jordan, Mr., 113–14

Kazin, Alfred, 73

Lady Chatterley's Lover, 15, 42
Lawrence, Arthur (father), 23; Law-
    rence's relationship to, 43, 45, 98,
    129
Lawrence, David Herbert: background
    of, 1, 73; Chambers's influence on,
    80–81; Freud's influence on, 1, 33,
    74–75; Hardy compared to, 1, 12;
    letters of, 30, 34, 44, 75, 76, 81,
    101; mysticism of, 73, 75, 78; as
    psychologist, 143, 152; and rela-
    tionship with father, 43, 45, 98,
    129; and relationship with mother,
    37, 44–45, 74, 75, 76, 77–78, 80,
    81, 91, 94; sexuality as viewed by,
    76–77, 78; Whitman's influence on,
    3; wife's (Frieda) influence on, 1,
    33, 80–81; as writer, 22, 71–73,
    104, 108, 128, 152
Lawrence, David Herbert, works of:
    characterization in, 76, 78, 136;
    general themes in, 21, 25, 132,
    144; men vs. women as theme in,
    136, 153; nature in, 12–13, 133–34;
    sexuality as theme in, 104, 133–34;
    style of, 6, 78, 136; vitality as
    theme in, 152, 153; weaknesses of,
    6, 72. See also specific works
Lawrence, Ernest (brother), 88
Lawrence, Frieda von Richthofen
    Weekley (wife), 1, 33, 80–81
Lawrence, Hardy, and American Literature
    (Swigg), 144
Lawrence, Lydia (mother), 23; death
    of, 78, 81; Lawrence's relationship
    with, 37, 44–45, 74, 75, 76, 77–78,
    80, 81, 91, 94
Leivers, Miriam: Clara Dawes com-
    pared to, 98, 99, 100, 150; frigidity
    of, 47–48, 95, 96; general charac-
    teristics of, 6, 90; Gertrude Morel's
    relationship to, 31–32, 35–36, 58,
    89, 139, 146, 149; lifelessness of,
    50, 59, 61, 68, 149, 151; as mother
    figure, 139, 140; Paul Morel's rela-
    tionship to, 6, 7, 17, 36, 47–48,
    53–55, 56–57, 58, 59–60, 61–63,
    64–69, 74, 75, 76, 81, 88–89, 92,

93–97, 98, 99, 134, 139–40, 149–
    50, 151; possessiveness of, 7, 17,
    36, 47, 57, 62, 63, 66–67, 89, 92,
    134, 139, 149, 150, 151; as pris-
    oner, 89, 93, 94, 126, 149; as pupil,
    51, 52, 53, 54, 55, 65; sensitivity
    of, 47, 51–53, 61; sexuality of, 16–
    17, 66, 85, 90, 93, 96; spirituality
    of, 47, 61, 134, 139; vitality of, 2,
    62, 66, 68, 90, 93, 95, 97

Malraux, André, 20
Man and Superman (Shaw), 71
Mann, Thomas, 21
Martz, Louis L., 2, 80, 84, 97
Meredith, George, 71
Miko, Stephen J., 144, 151, 152
Milton, John, 26
"Monologue of a Mother," 38
Morel, Annie, 38, 39–40, 148
Morel, Arthur, 15, 49, 94, 148
Morel, Gertrude: Clara Dawes's rela-
    tionship to, 36, 58, 98, 150; class
    consciousness of, 84–85, 86, 89,
    114–15; death of, 38–39, 40, 74,
    75, 107, 126, 137; general charac-
    teristics of, 25, 87, 91, 147; lan-
    guage of, 63, 115; lifelessness of,
    14, 90; as martyr, 25, 41, 90–91;
    Miriam Leivers's relationship to,
    31–32, 35–36, 58, 89, 139, 146,
    149; Paul Morel's relationship to,
    2, 6–7, 30–39, 40–41, 42, 43, 58–
    59, 67, 74, 75, 81–82, 84, 86, 87,
    88, 89, 90, 94, 95, 96, 97, 100–101,
    106, 122, 123, 134, 137–38, 141,
    144, 150, 151, 152; possessiveness
    of, 2, 7, 31–32, 35, 57–58, 59, 81,
    89, 106, 150; as prisoner, 114, 147;
    sexuality of, 29, 85; Walter Morel's
    relationship to, 7, 25, 27–30, 43–
    44, 63–64, 84, 85, 122–23, 124–
    25, 131, 137, 145–46, 147; William
    Morel's relationship to, 7, 84, 85,
    86–87
Morel, Paul: alienation of, 19–20, 139;
    Annie Morel's relationship to, 38,
    39–40; Baxter Dawes's relationship
    to, 4, 134, 135; Beatrice's relation-
    ship to, 65, 89; childishness of, 67,

92, 93, 94, 132, 133, 135, 139, 140; Clara Dawes's relationship to, 7, 15, 19, 74, 75, 76, 83, 97, 98–100, 106–7, 121, 132–34, 138–39; class consciousness of, 42–43, 86; death wish of, 135, 138, 141–42, 151; general characteristics of, 41, 64, 86, 87, 134, 151; Gertrude Morel's relationship to, 2, 6–7, 30–39, 40–41, 42, 43, 58–59, 67, 74, 75, 81–82, 84, 86, 87, 88, 89, 90, 94, 95, 96, 97, 100–101, 106, 122, 123, 134, 137–38, 141, 144, 150, 151, 152; killing of Gertrude Morel by, 38–39, 40, 126, 137; language of, 15, 49, 98, 125; lifelessness of, 60, 128–29; Miriam Leivers's relationship to, 6, 7, 17, 36, 47–48, 53–55, 56–57, 58, 59–60, 61–63, 64–69, 74, 75, 76, 81, 88–89, 92, 93–97, 98, 99, 134, 139–40, 149–50, 151; as prisoner, 36, 41, 57, 68, 76, 86, 88–89, 92, 93, 94, 98, 99, 100, 101, 114, 139, 144, 145, 146, 149–51; repression of, 35, 74, 76, 82–83, 85, 88, 90, 92, 94, 95, 106–7, 123; self-discovery of, 107, 132–33, 134; sexuality of, 74, 76, 82–83, 95, 96, 97, 98–99, 101, 106–7, 124, 131–32, 133; vitality of, 128–29, 138, 141, 148–49, 150, 151, 152; Walter Morel's relationship to, 6, 31, 32–34, 41–43, 49, 135

Morel, Walter: drunkenness of, 8, 9, 85, 87, 120, 121; general characteristics of, 49, 146; gentleness of, 33, 122, 125, 146; Gertrude Morel's relationship to, 7, 25, 27–30, 43–44, 63–64, 84, 85, 122–23, 124–25, 131, 137, 145–46, 147; language of, 15, 49, 115, 118, 119; Paul Morel's relationship to, 6, 31, 32–34, 41–43, 49, 135; sexuality of, 94, 132; vitality of, 13, 14–16, 20, 25, 26, 27, 41, 48–49, 64, 118, 119–20, 121, 125, 129, 135, 146

Morel, William: death of, 6, 20–21, 22, 81, 87, 88, 118, 148; general characteristics of, 117–18, 148; Gertrude Morel's relationship to, 7, 84, 85, 86–87; Louisa ("Gipsy") Western's relationship to, 86, 87–88,

118, 148; as prisoner, 94, 148

"Most Prevalent Form of Degradation in Erotic Life, The" (Freud), 74–75

Moynahan, Julian, 151

Nin, Anaïs, 152

O'Connor, Frank, 74

Paul Morel, 1. See also *Sons and Lovers*

Pride and Prejudice (Austen), 12

Rainbow, The, 150

Rees, Richard, 44

"Rex," 25

Rilke, Rainer Maria, 21

"Rocking-Horse Winner, The," 87, 88

Rowse, A. L., 37

Sanders, Scott, 152

Schorer, Mark, 37, 79, 80

Sons and Lovers: autobiographical elements in, 1–2, 3, 23–24, 30, 43–45, 55, 74, 75, 79, 80–81, 82, 87, 88, 91, 94, 101; background of, 1, 143; class consciousness as theme in, 3, 28, 42, 84–85, 115, 117, 118; coal mines in, 13–14, 112; darkness as symbol in, 18, 20–21, 22, 101, 134, 141; death as theme in, 21–22, 128, 132, 141; doll episode in, 39–41; flowers in, 9, 11, 16–18, 56–57, 60, 64, 66, 67, 85, 104–6, 107, 108, 126, 132; general themes in, 41, 126–27, 132, 144; *Hamlet* compared to, 123, 125–26, 152; hen episode in, 10–11, 50–51; history in, 111–13; homes in, 110–11, 113, 114, 120, 121; humor and irony in, 9, 92; imagery in, 7–9, 16, 43–44, 132; incest motif in, 7, 31, 32, 34, 58–59, 101, 106, 123, 137, 145; industrialization as theme in, 113, 114–15, 117, 121; Jordan's episodes in, 113–14, 115, 116, 120; language in, 119, 124, 126–28; love as theme in, 119, 128, 129, 144, 145; men

Sons and Lovers (continued)
vs. women as theme in, 120, 143–44; as metaphysical work, 73–74, 77; names in, 110; narrator's role in, 2, 48, 49, 53, 55–56, 60–61, 67, 79–80, 81–82, 84, 86, 87, 90, 91, 92–93, 94, 95–96, 97–98, 99, 100, 101, 106, 108, 136, 141; nature in, 11, 133–34; as oedipal work, 32–34, 59, 73–74, 77, 82, 87, 101, 123, 125–26, 135, 144, 151; phallic imagery in, 9–11, 20; railways in, 112–13; "Rocking-Horse Winner" compared to, 87, 88; sexuality as theme in, 7, 13, 18–19, 32, 83–84, 105, 107–8, 123–24, 125, 128, 131, 133–34; structure of, 6–7, 79, 80, 84, 88; style of, 2–4, 48, 52, 104–5, 108, 120, 138, 140; subjugation as theme in, 143–48, 152, 153; swing episode in, 50, 53; title of, 1; vitality as theme in, 16, 20, 144, 145, 148, 151, 152; weaknesses of, 3, 79, 123–25, 128, 136–37, 141–42, 144, 151; Women's Guild episodes in, 115–16, 117; women's roles in, 115–17, 118–19; work as theme in, 129, 139. *See also specific characters*
Spender, Stephen, 6, 22
Spilka, Mark, 47, 59

Study of Thomas Hardy, The, 44–45, 82
Swigg, Richard, 144

Taylor, Rachel Annand, 75, 76
Thackeray, William Makepeace, 71
Tindall, William York, 37
Tom Jones (Fielding), 11–12
Toward Women in Love (Miko), 151, 152
Trespasser, The, 143–44, 152
Trilling, Diana, 44
Troy, William, 72–73

Vivas, Eliseo, 37

Weiss, Daniel, 63, 74
West, Anthony, 39
Western, Louisa Lily Denys ("Gipsy"), 86, 87–88, 118, 148
White Peacock, The, 143–44
Whitman, Walt, 3
Wilson, Edmund, 133
Women in Love, 4
Woolf, Virginia, 71
Wuthering Heights (Brontë), 12

Yeats, William Butler, 71